Derby County's Hidden Treasures

RELICS OF THE RAMS

Derby County's Hidden Treasures

RELICS OF THE RAMS

BY ANDY ELLIS

breedon **books**
PUBLISHING

First published in Great Britain in 2005 by
The Breedon Books Publishing Company Limited
Breedon House, 3 The Parker Centre,
Derby, DE21 4SZ.

ISBN 1 85983 466 3

Printed and bound by Scotprint, Haddington.

Contents

Acknowledgements

It would be almost impossible for one person to accumulate all the items featured in this book, and many individuals have allowed me access to their prized possessions and memorabilia. Some of them are listed here and others do not wish to be identified individually. I thank all of them for their support and guidance and would like to especially mention my wife Jenny and daughters Naomi and Katie who have had to put up with me being locked away for many evenings and weekends during the last few months to work on this book. My thanks to: Geoff Burke, Tom Cooper, Alan and Hugh Cumming, John Ellis, Wilf Gerrard, Tony Hobson, Steve and Christopher Hudson, Nick Jellyman, Roy McFarland, Gary Maguire, Mick Perry, Mrs Barbara Robinson, Peter Seddon, Ian Stals, Paul Tattershaw, Keith Wilkinson and Jim Woolley.

Introduction

The word relic is defined as 'an object interesting because of its age or association' and that describes exactly what this book is about.

Within these pages you will find examples of many of the items associated with Derby County, from its formation in 1884 through to the present day. Some will be familiar and common pieces, others will be seen for the first time. These will include such diverse items as Baseball Ground turnstiles, the trophies on display at Pride Park Stadium, former players' personal collections and the matchday programmes.

The book is not meant to be a comprehensive catalogue of every programme, book and item available to purchase, but is a selective look at various objects. Some appear for sale on a regular basis and others are rarer and are shown from the club and various private collections.

Local auctions in early 2005 brought out various unique items of memorabilia dating from before World War One and these are likely to act as a catalyst for other old items to brought to auction in the Derby area.

The first football collectables that were found for sale in magazines such as *Charles Buchan's Football Monthly* and *Goal* were programmes. Full-time programme dealers appeared in the 1970s and produced mail-order catalogues. When the large auction houses such as Sotheby's and Christies began running regular football memorabilia auctions in the 1990s the prices of all types of memorabilia started escalating. With the downturn in the stock market, alternative investment markets such as antiques, wine and art were obvious targets for investors, but in recent years football memorabilia has been identified as a new area. Many older items and those with some historic sporting significance are purchased by investors as opposed to collectors, and this in turn has seen prices increase to over-inflated sums. While there is little chance of a price crash, prices may not carry on increasing at the same rate in the future.

Football memorabilia has thus become big business, with both full-time dealers and individuals trading on a part-time basis from their homes, using computers and internet auction sites to sell virtually anything to do with the sport. The internet has also opened markets across the globe and previously hidden and rare treasures have been found this way. The amount of memorabilia to show is largely determined by the on-field success of the team. This will become evident as you explore the years from 1950 through to the mid-1960s, when then club had a rather unspectacular period (just a Division Three North Championship to boast about) and rarely ventured far in the FA Cup competition. There was no demand for Derby County collectable material other than programmes. The arrival of the 1970s was a complete contrast, with trophies being won on a regular basis and many special and varied items being produced for people to collect.

Modern football clubs have their own marketing and merchandising operations with official club shops and, with greater media exposure, more merchandise has become available. In the last few years there has been a huge demand for printed material on the players, managers and history of the club.

It is only in the last 40 years or so that football items have become collectable, and people have bought and sold items for their own collection. Before then, any items that were kept were done so as a personal reminder of a trip made to a particular event or special publication to mark an on-the-field success. Programmes in most clubs up until the late 1960s were nothing more than a list of the players, a fixture list, League table, a few editorial notes and the occasional black and white picture, and were not produced with a view to them being kept as long-term souvenirs or, in some cases, investments. Even in the late 1940s spectators were encouraged to throw away their programmes on exiting the grounds so that the paper could be recycled.

For this reason, material prior to 1950 is getting increasingly rare, hard to obtain and quite expensive, and the further back into the 20th century and the latter part of the 19th century material is even more scarce.

I hope that you enjoy the nostalgia and history that accompany the pictures of the trophies and artefacts featured in this book. Many of these exist in personal collections, not only in Derbyshire but from as far away as Canada and Australia, and are rarely seen outside those personal environments.

It would be nice to think that at some point in the future an official Derby County Museum or Hall of Fame based at Pride Park could be built to house a central repository of programmes, historic documents, medals, caps and many of the items shown in these pages. There they would be on permanent loan to the club, stored safely and displayed for the public to see.

Andy Ellis
August 2005

You will not find any prices against any of the items shown in these pages because:

- some of the items will be unique and by definition almost impossible to price
- the condition of any item can greatly affect its value (e.g. if one takes a match programme and then writes on all the team changes, scorers and attendance it will have much less of a value than one without the writing)
- there are two prices that could be quoted: one as an insurance value (i.e. what it would cost to replace the item with a similar one); and one for what you might expect to receive by selling it privately, although by selling it to a football memorabilia trader you will not be offered its true value.
- prices change constantly and would put this book out of date immediately (consider what would have happened had this book been published on the Monday morning of Brian Clough's death, showing the values of his books and autographs. By the afternoon the prices of these would have increased dramatically).

Chapter One
The Early Years
1884-1919

Derby County Football Club was originally formed as an offshoot of the county cricket club to help boost the ailing finances and playing fortunes of the club. Organised football was still in its infancy in England but the games that had taken place had seen much public support, particularly among working-class men, and the cricket club wished to exploit this new interest.

The links with the cricket club were strong. Initially they shared players, facilities, team colours (amber, chocolate and pale blue) and originally even the same name – Derbyshire County Football Club. The county Football Association objected to this choice of name as it implied it was representative of the county as a whole and should have the name of the place, so it was shortened to Derby County.

The first match for the football club was an away game against Great Lever on 13 September 1884, which ended in a rather disappointing 6–0 defeat, with John Goodall, who was later to join Derby, scoring four goals. Two weeks later the first home fixture was staged and the famous Blackburn Olympic, who were the current FA Cup holders and the team credited with breaking the dominance of public schools, were the visitors. For this prestigious match, Derby brought in a number of guest players to help launch the new club in the town (another football team called Derby Midland had been in existence and was the leading club in the area), and Benjamin Spilsbury scored the first-ever goal by Derby County within the first five minutes. Despite this, the Olympic team ran out 4–3 winners, but the first victory was secured on 1 November in the Derbyshire Cup against St Luke's.

After four years of mainly friendly matches, the first professional League was formed, with all 12 teams being based north of Birmingham and the first League game for Derby being at Bolton on 8 September 1888. After a faltering start that had Bolton leading 3–0, the Derby team was level by half-time and added a further three goals in the second period.

These early years in the Football League saw the club mainly finishing nearer the bottom than the top, and they had to re-apply for re-election to the League on a number of occasions as they tried to compete with clubs who had been in existence for much longer and had greater financial budgets to attract the more famous names.

The Derby Midland football club was taken over in 1891 and as part of that all the players joined the staff of Derby County, giving a larger pool of players to choose from.

The famous Preston North End and England player John Goodall was persuaded to join Derby in 1889 and his experience and on-field influence was to have an effect.

By 1892 a young Steve Bloomer had been given a chance to play in the first team, more by accident than design, as three players from the previous season were not re-registered in time to play in the first League game of the season at Stoke.

The first official manager/secretary was Harry Newbould, who had been a former player, and he saw them through these early, difficult years.

With Bloomer in the team, the club made great strides forward, moving permanently to the Baseball Ground in 1895 with the help of Sir Francis Ley, and reached three FA Cup Finals in 1898, 1899 and 1903, losing all of them, the last one being the heaviest defeat in a Final to this day, a 6–0 reverse at the hands of Bury.

Following Bloomer's surprising transfer to Middlesbrough during the summer of 1907, the club was relegated to Division Two where it remained for five seasons, until he was brought back and continued scoring goals for the Rams.

By the start of World War One, the first 30 years had been eventful and had seen Derby County Football Club establish itself in a football town, have some of the most famous players the English game had ever known in John Goodall and Steve Bloomer, appear in three Cup Finals and five other semi-finals and suffer relegation and promotion.

Books

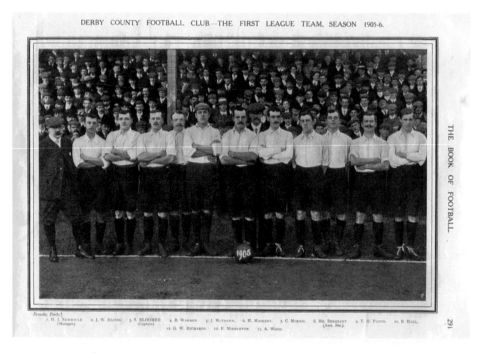

DERBY COUNTY FOOTBALL CLUB—THE FIRST LEAGUE TEAM, SEASON 1905-6.

In contrast to today's seemingly non-stop production of football books, publications in the early years of the Football League and football clubs in general were virtually non-existent. This was for a number of reasons, primarily that there was little or no historical material to base any book upon, there was not the widespread interest in any particular club to justify production of printed history and the game was expanding and evolving so quickly that writers were not able to keep pace. The majority of the first football books, therefore, were instructional in their nature, explaining how to play the game and its various facets.

Association Football and The Men Who Made It (1907) was a huge production for its time and was published in four volumes, with over 200 pages in each, and was the first definitive history of the game. Each volume was lavishly illustrated with photographic plates and often it is these pictures, instead of the whole book, which are very valuable.

Within the pages of Volume Two is the first written history of Derby County, supplemented by a team photograph of 1905–06. One section of the book features 'Giants of the Game' and includes Bloomer and John Goodall, and another, 'The Forward Game', is written by Bloomer himself.

Football annuals covering all the Leagues, major competitions and clubs have appeared since the 1870s, and publishers of these early works include Cope's, *The Athletic News*, Gamage's and *News of the World*, but it was not until clubs reached their 50th anniversary that any form of specific club history was written to mark the occasion.

Newspapers

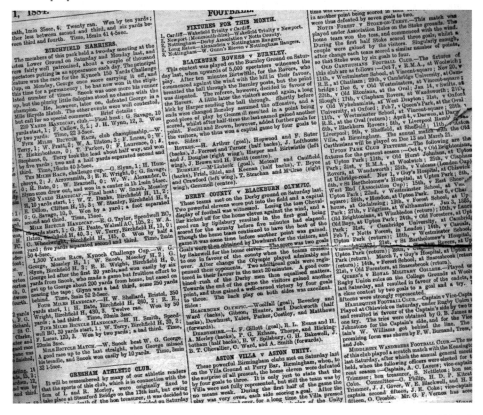

Newspapers have often been used as good reference material for research into the early football matches, but often two or three reports of the same game need to be studied to confirm details as there was a great deal of mis-identification of players and scorers in those early games (there were no shirt numbers until 1966 and programmes were very rarely produced).

The early match reports make interesting reading with their terminology and descriptions. One such rare example is this original newspaper, *Bell's Life in London and Sporting Chronicle*, dated 1 October 1884, which contains a match report of Derby's first-ever home game against Blackburn Olympic, where the Derby team is named as both Derby County and Derbyshire.

Copies of similar early match reports can be obtained from the local studies library or the British Newspaper Library at Colindale in London, but originals are extremely rare.

J. Nib was a cartoonist for the *Derby Express* newspaper in around 1908–09 and large numbers

of his original pen drawings were sold in the mid-1980s and also resold in the autumn of 2001. These large drawings, measuring over 10 x 8 inches, are all signed and dated by the artist and many have a handwritten comment on the reverse.

This example on the left is entitled 'Big Game Hunting', with the comment that Derby County meet West Bromwich Albion next Saturday.

Colours

As Derby County started life as part of the cricket club, it was natural that they should adopt the same colours – chocolate, amber and blue – but as there are no colour photographs available of these early teams it is difficult to accurately say in what combination they were used, but by looking at one of the earliest known, and very rarely seen, pictures of the team prior to their first home game, it is possible to work out from the lightness of the parts of the shirt that they were chocolate and blue halves with amber sleeves (opposite page, top).

As the football and cricket clubs began to operate independently, naturally the football club wished to establish its own identity further and, in common with many clubs of the era, the playing strip regularly changed until a combination of colours was settled on that became known locally and nationally as belonging to the club. The goalkeeper would also wear the same coloured shirt as the other players, but could be identified in photographs as he would often wear a cap.

Derby appeared to go through seasons when they wore an all-black kit, stripes and the traditional white shirts. However, over time the white shirts and black shorts prevailed, and, as with many other clubs, the more basic and simple kits were more likely to be used on a permanent basis. Blackburn Rovers probably have the oldest kit design. Their blue and white halves have remained unchanged from the original shirts.

THE DAILY GRAPHIC FOOTBALL ALBUM, 1904-1905.   3

First row : H. J. Newbould (Secretary-Manager), Geo. Davis, R. Warren, J. Methven, P. Hall, H. Maskery, C. Morris, C. Richards, A. Latham (Trainer), E. Ratcliffe.
Second row : R. E. Hounsfield, S. Bloomer (Captain), T. H. Paton, T. Fletcher, J. Moore, A. McAllister.

DERBY COUNTY.

Photographed by Dereski, Derby.

A modern book, *Football Colours*, shows a number of different designs and colours, although there is no knowing how this information was obtained. There were no programmes to refer to and no colour pictures to substantiate the author's drawings. Included was one in red and blue, but another source shows it as red and blue stripes. There are no known pictures of any such playing strip.

John Goodall's shirt from the 1893–94 season shows that the shirts were actually scarlet and white halves on the front and back. It was previously thought that the shirts were black and white halves, as that is how it seems from the black and white photographs. Contemporary newspaper reports suggest that this scarlet kit was used throughout that season.

The programmes from the FA Cup Finals of the era suggest that a number of different coloured kits were used – white against Nottingham Forest in 1898 and Sheffield United in 1899 and red against Bury in 1903. Contemporary magazines and newspapers are not reliable enough as they mainly carried drawings and artists' interpretations of the action in lieu of the photography we have become accustomed to today. Some of those drawings were coloured and often gave a false impression of the true team colours used.

Stadium: The Racecourse

A stadium is too grand a word to describe the place where the early football matches were played. They were not the modern shiny steel and concrete structures we are used to seeing today, but more than likely a pitch marked out with a rope around to keep the spectators back and nothing more than a cinder bank for terracing. The changing rooms would have been in a timber pavilion. Derby's first football pitch was situated at its original base at the Racecourse Ground, which is still used by Derbyshire County Cricket Club today.

In research done by Dave Twydell for his book *Grounds for a Change*, the exact location of the first Derby County football field is marked on a map of the Racecourse. The pitch seems to have been

in the area where the new scoreboard has been built, running parallel with Sir Frank Whittle Way. Derby's first home game was in 1884 against the mighty Blackburn Olympic team and drew an attendance of 1,500. Admission was 2½ pence, with ladies admitted free. The entrance to the football field was by the canal bridge.

Horse racing had been taking place at the Racecourse since the early 19th century and inevitably a race meeting would sooner or later clash with the expanding football fixture list. As football was the emerging and less well-established sport, it was the football match that had to be rescheduled or relocated.

A fixture against Sunderland on 19 March 1892 was the first of these rearranged matches and was played on a plot of land adjacent to Sir Francis Ley's factory, which he had converted into playing fields for his staff. Sir Francis Ley was widely travelled and had brought back the game of baseball to the UK and set up a local team to take part in the English league. Part of the football pitch crossed the baseball field, which became known as Catcher's Corner (the area that joined the Popside with the Osmaston End).

Although the playing surface at the Racecourse was far superior to that of Ley's playing fields, the players preferred the new surroundings as the wide, open expanse of the Racecourse would often make for a very cold and windswept game of football.

As football became more popular, with a steady rise in attendances, an increasing fixture list would cause more clashes with the horse racing and a long-term solution had to be found.

The facilities were not great at the Racecourse, with the Pavilion offering the only source of comfort for any spectator, and although the original grandstand (demolished in 1911) could have been used it was too far away for spectators to get a good view. Despite these disadvantages, Derby had already staged five FA Cup semi-final matches as well as a FA Cup Final replay in 1886 between Blackburn Rovers and West Bromwich Albion. The major reason Derby was chosen for these matches was not because of the facilities, but because Derby was located centrally between the opponents and had a major railway line.

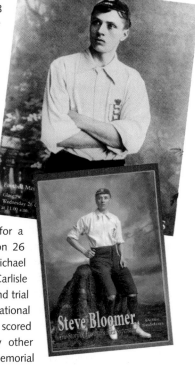

In 1895 Sir Francis Ley offered the use of his land to the football club and even paid for and moved the existing wooden stands and equipment a couple of miles across the city. The first match at the new permanent home, known as the Baseball & Football Ground, was also against Sunderland on 14 September 1895. It is highly unlikely that any special commemorative items were produced to mark the event.

Bloomer

Steve Bloomer's life and career is detailed superbly in Peter Seddon's book, *Steve Bloomer: The Story of Football's First Superstar*, published by Breedon Books in 1999. What makes this a remarkable piece of work is the fact that Bloomer died in 1938 and the author has had to rely on contemporary newspaper reports, extensive library research and the cooperation of Bloomer's grandson, Steve Richards. The book has many photographs of Bloomer in his latter years and contains details of his time coaching in Germany and Spain.

Interest in football history has increased dramatically in the last 20 years and fans have begun to learn about the stars of long ago. Items relating to the Bloomer years at Derby remain elusive to the private collector and there is little to be found that bears his name or relates to him. Items that do come into the public domain are keenly sought after by football fans everywhere, who recognise him as one of the all-time greats.

Bloomer's family did sell some items to raise money for a memorial to be built in Derby, and this sale took place on 26 October 1994 at Christies auction house in Glasgow. Mr Michael Knighton, a Derbyshire-born man and former chairman of Carlisle United, paid a bargain price of £8,000 for 19 international and trial caps dating from 1895 (the year of Bloomer's first international against Ireland, which was played at Derby, and in which he scored two goals in a 9–0 victory) to 1907, along with many other newspaper cuttings and articles relating to Bloomer. The memorial

STEVE BLOOMER
ENGLAND'S GREATEST INTERNATIONAL FOOTBALL PLAYER & RECORD CAP HOLDER.
INTERNATIONAL CAPS
SCOTLAND. 1895, 97, 98, 99, 1900, 01, 02, 04, 05.
WALES. 1896, 97, 99, 1901, 02, 05.
IRELAND. 1895, 96, 97, 99, 1902, 05.
ENGLISH BADGE   GERMAN BADGE

was unveiled in central Derby in October 1996.

The resurgent interest in all football history has turned the spotlight back on Bloomer, as Derby's greatest player, and a fund to get a permanent statue erected at Pride Park was launched in 2004.

As you would expect, the wages of the playing staff today are significantly different from those in the early days, and the Players Committee Book for 1900–01 shows that Bloomer was paid £5 per week during both the summer and winter months. The next most highly-paid player was James Methven, who received £3 10s.

A later note from the meeting of the Players Committee on 2 October 1901 says 'Bloomer was in attendance and apologised for insobriety and inattention to training. He was severely admonished by the Committee and on giving an undertaking to behave better in the future it was resolved he be not fined'.

Bloomer has also been pictured as part of the Derby baseball team, which started playing in May 1890 and was probably the

to the
UNVEILING
of the
STEVE BLOOMER MEMORIAL

A Monument to Honour the
Late England, Derby County
and Middlesbrough Star

at

LOCK-UP YARD
CORNMARKET, DERBY

on

Monday, 28 October, 1996

and to

THE CITY COUNCIL'S
ASSEMBLY ROOMS
('45 Suite)
MARKET PLACE
For Drinks and Buffet

Schedule:

Cocktails 12.30 - 1.30
('45 Suite)

Unveiling 1.40 - 2.00
(Lock-Up Yard)

Reception 2.15
('45 Suite)

RSVP
by 21 October

Steve Richards
4 Lodge Cottage, Sandypits Lane,
Etwall, Nr. Derby. DE65 6JA

Mobile: (0589) 955923

Note: Lifts and Parking at Assembly Rooms

STEVE BLOOMER

THE

GREATEST

goalscorer in

Derby County Football Club

History ....

best baseball team in the country. He was part of the side that defeated the American champions, the Boston Beaneaters.

Little remains of Derby's baseball history, with the City Museum holding the majority of the collection.

Cigarette and Trade cards

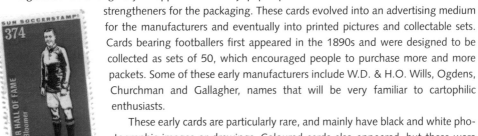

Cigarettes were originally wrapped in a flimsy paper packet and blank cards were inserted as strengtheners for the packaging. These cards evolved into an advertising medium for the manufacturers and eventually into printed pictures and collectable sets. Cards bearing footballers first appeared in the 1890s and were designed to be collected as sets of 50, which encouraged people to purchase more and more packets. Some of these early manufacturers include W.D. & H.O. Wills, Ogdens, Churchman and Gallagher, names that will be very familiar to cartophilic enthusiasts.

These early cards are particularly rare, and mainly have black and white photographic images or drawings. Coloured cards also appeared, but these were drawings as the concept of colour photography was still some years away.

A very famous set of collector cards was produced by John Baines from Manningham, Bradford, from 1887 onwards. These were very colourful cards and were often produced in a shield or football shape, concentrating on clubs based in the North and Midlands. They were sold in packs of six for half a penny and were avidly collected by schoolboys. Their popularity allowed commercial businesses to start promoting their products on the backs of the cards. The colours of these cards and their unique shapes make them highly collectable and they are very expensive to purchase, even as single cards.

Early Cup Finals

Derby had appeared in three FA Cup Finals (losing all of them) in their first 20 years of existence, the 1903 Final against Bury being their heaviest defeat (6–0).

The amount of collectable material from these early Finals is very limited, and as a consequence the prices will reflect their rarity if they were ever to appear at auction.

In 2003 copies of the three FA Cup Final programmes were sold at a Sotheby's auction for a total of £21,120, despite them being incomplete and in generally poor condition. The 1899 programme against Sheffield United, which was the most complete of the three, was responsible for over half of that total. Financially, these items are beyond the means of most collectors, but an alternative way of obtaining these items is to purchase reproductions of them and associated material from these games.

These reproductions carry none of the associated high insurance risks, are printed on modern quality paper and can be handled without fear of causing damage. Examples that are readily available are the 1903 programme and various prints taken from contemporary magazines and newspapers giving the story of the game in drawings, as action photographs were not possible at the time. However, as these were artists' impressions of the game and major incidents, they should be treated with caution.

There is also, although it is very rare, a souvenir programme from the 1903 Final, which has the trophy on the front cover and the teams inside.

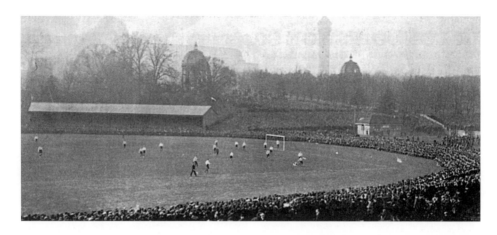

A postcard (page 25, top right) was very quickly produced in the Bury area following their Cup victory on 18 April. It shows a Derby player falling over having eaten too much Bury pudding, with the Cup displayed in the shop window behind. The postcard is stamped in New York on 29 April and again in Barbados on 9 May.

To find a match ticket from before World War Two is rare enough, so to have a ticket from the 1899 FA Cup Final against Sheffield United, played at Crystal Palace, is extraordinary (page 25, middle). To attend a Cup Final today, one would expect to pay more for a ticket than a normal League fixture and this practice was evident even in the 19th century. The price on the ticket is 5 shillings for the Final alone and a season ticket for all Derby home games for the whole

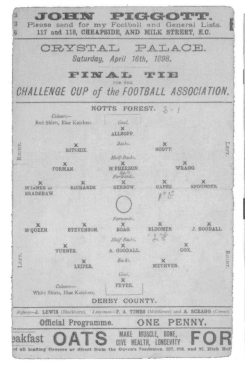

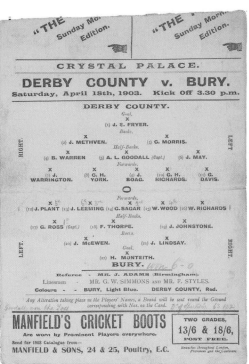

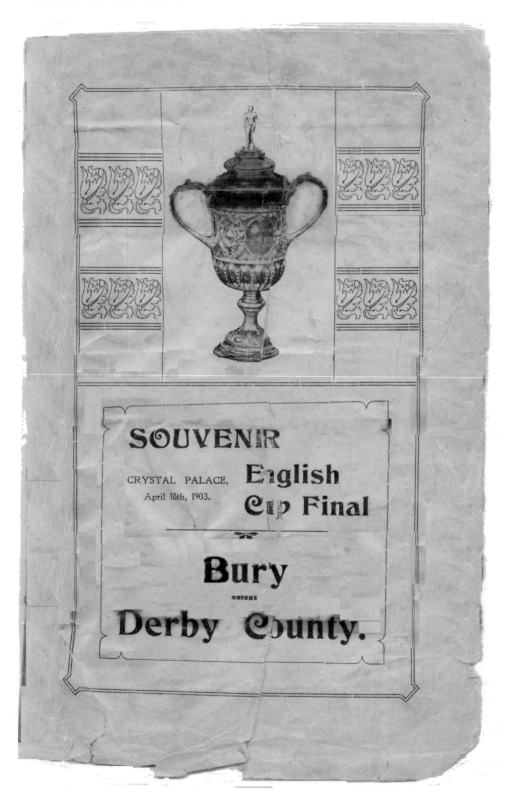

© The National
Football Museum

THE FOOTBALL
ASSOCIATION.

Derby County
v.
Millwall,
MARCH 21st, 1903.

STEWARD.

season was just over double that price. The match ball from this game is in Sheffield United's Hall of Fame exhibition at Bramall Lane.

The record-breaking FA Cup Final of 1903, which saw the Bury team win by a record winning margin of 6–0, is still celebrated in the Lancashire town, but there are a few pieces of memorabilia relating to the game that survive. Unusually, one is the match ball, which is on display at the National Football Museum in Preston. It is now quite shrivelled and patched and has the score painted on it.

Other items include the runners'-up medal awarded to John Boag, one of only three players (Fryer and Methven being the others) to have played in all three of those early Finals. Unusually, the medal has his name engraved on the back, which has to have been done after the game.

Derby played Millwall in the semi-final of the 1903 competition, and the stewards appointed by the Football Association for the game were issued with special ribbons to identify themselves. These days they would be wearing the bright yellow, fluorescent jackets.

Season tickets and Tickets

The earliest known season ticket dates from the 1888–89 season, the first season of League football. It is nothing special to look at on the outside and cost 7s 6d. For this the owner would be allowed admission 'to Ground and Pavilion to all County matches.' Inside is the club's fixture list for that first, historic League season, which also includes fixtures for the Derbyshire County representative team.

This season ticket was sold by Nottingham auctioneers Vennett-Smith at their auction in November 2004 and remains in private hands, but the football club has two season ticket books, one from the 1896–97 season (owned by J. Moore of 208 Burton Road) and one from the 1905–06

D.C.F.C., Ltd.

A. C. or D.

SEASON
1905-6.

SUBSCRIBER.
12/6

season (owned by J. Lowe of 64 Regent Street), both in remarkably good condition. The price of both tickets is the same at 12s 6d for the season, and for this admittance was allowed to the 'A' and 'C' pavilions as well as the Osmaston Road End. The 1896–97 ticket opens out to

DERBY COUNTY F.C.,
LIMITED.

SHAREHOLDER
£1 10s. 0d.

SEASON
1913-14. ALL STANDS

reveal the fixtures for the club and the admittance rules, and the club officials are listed on the folded out portions.

By the 1913-14 season prices had risen steadily to £1 10s for the season.

Paper napkin

This paper napkin dates from the FA Cup tie between Derby and Nottingham Forest, played on 6 March 1909. It was printed by Macmillan Litho of Derby and is a unique souvenir from the game. There are no records of what it would have been used for, but it was possibly from a pre-match dinner or was a souvenir given away outside the ground prior to the game.

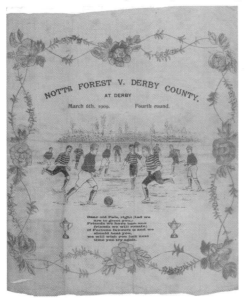

Unusually, Notts Forest are mentioned first on the napkin, and the team playing against them in the picture are playing in hoops – which Derby have never done – while the Forest team are the ones in coloured shirts. This might indicate that it was produced for the Nottingham-based supporters.

The writing on the napkin gives no mention of either team and this could indicate that the product is a multi-purpose one. By changing the fixture details at the top and the colour of the shirts the napkins could be sold at different venues.

Napkins similar to this were often produced for Cup Finals and are often seen at various auctions, but they do not often relate to the earlier rounds of the competition.

Programmes

As with any printed material from these early years, programmes are particularly rare for Derby County matches, especially home games, with few examples to refer to. According to the leading programme collecting publication in the UK, *Programme Monthly*, the earliest example of a Derby County home programme is from 5 September 1903, for the fixture against Wolverhampton Wanderers. The format of the card or programme was the same for a number of years, showing drawings of the players on the front with their names underneath.

This is not always the case as teams such as Aston Villa, Chelsea, Sheffield United and Sheffield Wednesday produced bound volumes of programmes for those wealthy enough to be able to afford them. During the intervening years, these have been split to remove the binding, so leaving the individual programmes that can be sold. These programmes, although still rare, do appear quite regularly for sale and can be purchased for a reasonable cost and are generally in good condition for items over 100 years old.

A number of these early programmes have also been reprinted, usually by clubs who are celebrating an anniversary. These reproductions are well worth the minimal cost as they are printed on modern paper and one can appreciate the programme without worrying about handling it.

The first Sheffield United programme ever issued was against Derby on 1 September 1897 and this was re-printed in 1989 and was included free in the Sheffield United v Reading programme of that year to mark the centenary of the Yorkshire club.

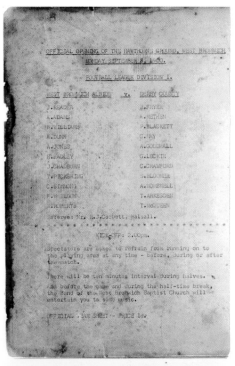

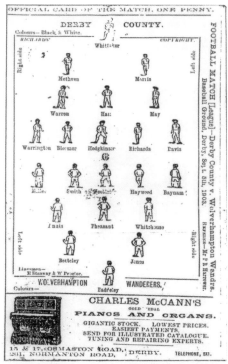

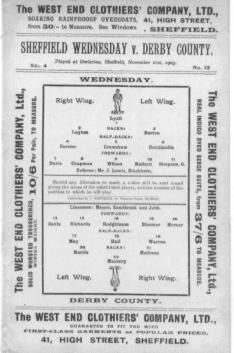

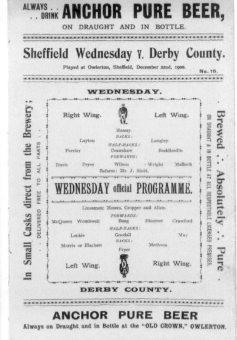

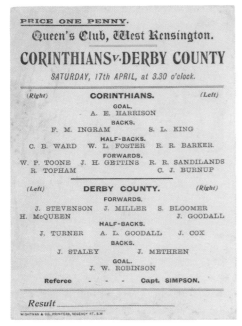

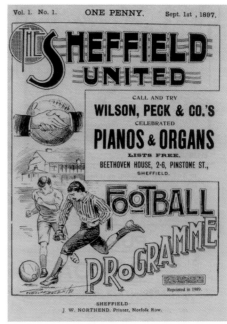

The West Bromwich Albion programme, by contrast, is nothing more than a sheet listing the teams for the first game played at the Hawthorns ground in September 1900. This example is included in the West Bromwich Albion Memorabilia Pack from 2002.

Other examples shown are: Bristol City, FA Cup semi-final at Chelsea in 1909; Corinthians 1896 friendly match, Sheffield Wednesday Reserves 1902, Sheffield Wednesday 1900.

Toy figures

A set of 11 die-cast lead players was produced by Wm. Britains Ltd in their civilian toy series. The company are better known for producing lead figures depicting armies of the world and farmyard figures. These figures are 2½ inches (54mm) high and a full set consists of a goalkeeper (standing), two full-backs (walking), three half-backs (trotting) and five forwards (running). These are extremely hard to find, even as individual players, and it is almost impossible to collect a full team. This team of Derby players was manufactured in 1904, set 181b, along with 11 other major teams of the day, and a further 16 teams were added in 1934. There is no way of telling if a figure is part of the 1904 or 1934 sets as they were made from the same mould, but the early figures did have a paper sticker on with the date, but that nearly always came off. The goalkeeper figure is the best way of telling the age. The early ones were usually painted in exactly the same shirt colour as the rest of the players, whereas the later ones

would have a coloured shirt (green, red or blue). The examples shown are the full-back and goalkeeper from the 1904 set.

Postcards

Postcards were very popular in the early football years, some produced as part of a set, some produced for specific matches and others showing the famous players of the day. Postcard collectors are also very keen to obtain early examples, regardless of the subject matter.

John Goodall, breasting the ball, is featured as one of a set of six photographic postcards featuring famous players and showing different skills, produced around 1900 and printed in Germany, and featured in the FIFA Museum Collection book.

A further example is for Derby's visit to Woolwich Arsenal on 18 March 1905, during which Derby were expected to be heavily beaten. The result of 0–0 prompted the cartoon to be printed in the *Kentish Independent* and subsequently on a postcard, now at Pride Park Stadium. The narrative says 'Now I've got you here I'm blessed if my knife is sharp enough to do the job decent like. You'd better go home and come again when I've got it sharpened.'

Ben Warren was granted a testimonial match and this was against Newhall Swifts Past and Present, where he started his career, on 30 April 1914. One side of the card has a picture of the player with his playing record and caps, while the reverse has details of the match. Whether this was a promotional card to publicise the game or a souvenir from the match itself is unclear.

Team Photos/Photographic plates

The earliest known, and only, photographic plate showing a Derby County team in the original kit is shown on page 15, and from the various shading and tones on the picture one can see that the shirts were blue and chocolate halves with amber sleeves. This picture is taken outside the original double-fronted (football one side and cricket on the other) football and cricket pavilion at the Racecourse and is taken before Derby's first-ever home League game against West Bromwich Albion on 15 September 1888. The players in the picture are (from left to right) Marshall, Latham, Ferguson, Williamson, Monks, Roulstone, Bakewell, Cooper, Higgins and Plackett, the goalkeeper being identified by the fact that he is holding a pair of gloves. This was taken by Roberts & Sons of Holborn House, Nottingham Road, Derby.

There are many other examples of early plates, some used in the famous football books of the day and others used in magazines.

This early, rare action photo shows John Boag throwing the ball to Steve Bloomer; unfortunately the opposition and venue are unknown. It is undated, but would be prior to 1904 and possibly during the 1899 FA Cup Final against Sheffield United at the Crystal Palace.

Other pictures can be found in various magazines of the time:
Supplement to *Sports* magazine, dated 17 February 1896, which shows the Derby team in casual clothes, with Steve Bloomer lying on the floor.

The *Daily Graphic Football Album* shows Derby in a striped kit (colours unknown, could be black, red or blue) from 1904–05.

DERBY COUNTY FOOTBALL TEAM, 1895-6.

John Goodall

John Goodall was one of England's finest players in the 1890s, and he rose to fame by playing in the 'Invincibles' team of Preston North End that was undefeated for a season. Prior to that he had played for Great Lever and had scored four times against Derby in their first-ever competitive match. He is credited with aiding the young Steve Bloomer in some of the techniques and tactics of the game,

THE DAILY GRAPHIC FOOTBALL ALBUM, 1904-1905.   3

First row : H. J. Newbould (Secretary-Manager), Geo. Davis, R. Warren, J. Methven, R. Hall, H. Maskery, C. Morris, C. Richards, A. Latham (Trainer), E. Ratcliffe.
Second row : R. E. Hounsfield, S. Bloomer (Captain), T. H. Paton, T. Fletcher, J. Moore, A. McAllister.

DERBY COUNTY.

Photographed by Dereskf, Derby.

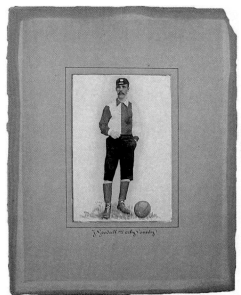

and they made a formidable partnership in the forward line.

One of his original Derby shirts, dating from 1893, still survives in the hands of the family and is in remarkably good condition. It still shows some grass stains (see club kit section).

The portrait of him shows the shirt with the colours in the opposite positions, but closer inspection of a contemporary team photograph shows a number of players wearing shirts with different designs (i.e. some where the left is scarlet and some where the right is scarlet).

Goodall was also an England international, despite his Scottish accent, captaining the national team twice in his 14 appearances for the country. Two of his caps are shown here, carrying multiple dates for the years he played.

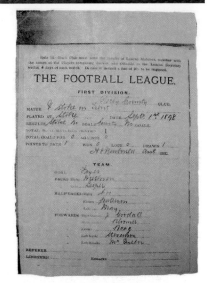

The Bass Charity Vase, in which the club still competes today, was being played for in Goodall's time, and his winners' medal from the 1891 competition is still retained by the family. Made from 9ct gold, it is hallmarked and was made in Birmingham.

Goodall's brother Archie also played over 400 times for Derby (but unusually he played international football for Northern Ireland) before moving to Plymouth Argyle in 1903.

The official record of the team that played at Stoke in a 0–0 draw on 1 September 1898 shows Goodall playing alongside Bloomer.

Autographs

The hobby of autograph hunting and collecting did not really start until after World War One and as such it is unusual to find an autograph page that dates from before 1920. This one is dated 1913 and has 13 autographs. Some of these are those of the players in the Division Two Championship team, and there are also those of trainer Arthur Latham and former player and then manager James Methven. The page also carries the autograph of Steve Bloomer, who would have been in his last playing season. In common with other examples of his autograph, he has written it at 90 degrees to the other players and put a full stop after 'Steve'. This would date the page to before February 1914, as Bloomer played his last game in January of that year.

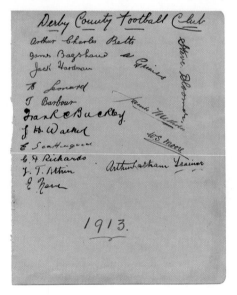

Fixture card

The club's first year in existence is detailed in a fixture card for the 1884–85 season. This small card has the first and second-team fixtures on the inside and, unusually, the back cover shows the Rugby rules. Under the first team the card shows 'Association Rules'. Although many sources say that the first victory was secured against St Luke's, this fixture card includes a handwritten fixture before that game, against Repton School, which was won 3–2.

Memorandum and Articles of Association

Incorporated on 14 August 1896 and updated and reprinted regularly afterwards, each and every club that has shareholders has to produce such a document to define the rules under which the club operates.

Under Clause 3, subsection 2,

the club would promote the practice and play of football, cricket, baseball, lacrosse, lawn tennis, hockey, bowls, bicycle and tricycle riding, running and jumping.

Disqualification of directors includes a Clause E – is found lunatic or becomes of unsound mind (how many directors in the last 120 years fall into that category?!)

The original share issue was just 5,000 shares of £1 each, and the first seven shareholders were listed together with their addresses and occupation (from a surgical bandage manufacturer to a grocer).

Share certificate

To raise funds for the club, people were able to purchase shares, each person being given a certificate in their name confirming their ownership. These certificates changed little in layout and general wording over the following 90 years, after which the

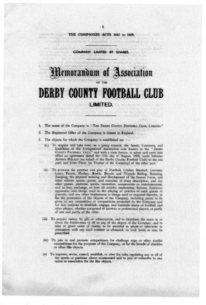

last ones were issued. The club has since gone back into private ownership, meaning that any shares became worthless in value, but the certificates are an interesting item to own. The example shown is from 1906 and belonged to Henry James Newbould of 2 Market Place, Derby. Mr Newbould was also the club secretary and the club's first recognised manager. He has signed the certificate in that capacity.

Another one of the first certificates (number 111) was sold to a person living in the shadow of the Baseball Ground at 99 Shaftesbury Crescent and dated 30 November 1896.

Chapter Two
The Inter-war Years
1920–1939

After securing promotion in the last season before World War One, Derby started in the First Division after the conflict and for the most part struggled, finishing a disappointing 18th, despite leading the table early on. The major problem faced by the team was that it was an ageing squad of players lacking a top-quality centre-forward. A lack of goals was to prove costly in the 1920–21 season as the 32 goals from 42 games was not enough to keep them in the Division.

A change of Division, a flurry of transfer activity and the inclusion of many young players did not help the Rams as they finished the following season in their lowest-ever League position of 12th in Division Two. Cecil Potter was brought in as manager from Hartlepools United and, despite another low finish of 14th in Division Two, an FA Cup semi-final appearance in 1923 nearly saw Derby appear in the famous 'white horse' Final, the first to be played at the new Wembley Stadium. Unfortunately, on the day, many players did not play as well as they could and the Rams were soundly beaten 5–2 by West Ham United.

The following two seasons saw a big change in fortunes. In 1923–24 Derby finished in third place. This placing was decided in the very last game of the season, in which Derby had to win 5–0 against Leicester City to gain promotion. Having won 4–0 (they were unable to score again in the last 25 minutes) they missed second place, and promotion, by one goal. It was during this season that Derby's record away victory was secured, an 8–0 win at Bristol City, with Harry Storer scoring four goals. Promotion was also nearly secured in the 1924–25 season as Derby spent much of it in the top two positions, slipping down to third with just two games to play.

By the 1925–26 season, George Jobey had been appointed manager and he had brought in Harry Bedford from Blackpool (he became the club's leading scorer for five successive seasons) and Tommy Cooper from Port Vale (later England's captain). Joining forces with established players such as George Thornewell and Harry Storer, the club gained promotion back to the First Division and a period of relative success followed, although there was no trophy to mark their achievements.

In December 1927 a new attendance record was set at the Baseball Ground with 30,858 crammed in for the visit of Bolton Wanderers, the remodelled Railway Terrace (otherwise known as the Popular Side) allowing more spectators in safely. Sammy Crooks was signed towards the end of the season, yet another player that was to play for many years and also become an England international.

The following seasons were the best the club had ever known, as they finished fourth, sixth and second and also brought in unknown players that were to become internationals a few years later – Barker and Bowers. There was a hint of unrest among the fans because the club did not go one step further and buy some new players that would provide adequate cover for injuries. The reserve team, which was not thought to be strong enough, actually finished in second place in the Central League but was, for the most part, neglected.

In fact the lowest finish until the outbreak of World War Two was a 15th place in 1932. In 1936 the team took another runners'-up spot without making a serious challenge for the Championship, with a team containing Hughie Gallagher, Dally Duncan, Sammy Crooks and Jack Nicholas. They were to reach another FA Cup semi-final, this time losing to Manchester City, but along the way they created a record attendance for the tie at Sunderland; over 75,000 were in the ground with many being locked out.

Cigarette cards

The period between 1920 and 1940 saw the number of cigarette cards produced reach its maximum, both in terms of quantity and quality. Seeing the success of cigarette cards, manufacturers of other products, particularly boys' magazines and sweets, began to produce similar cards, which have become known as 'trade cards' and for many years were thought of as being inferior to the cigarette cards previously produced and collected, but are of a similar quality and collectability. Collecting cards, of either type, was the first football memorabilia hobby that became organised across the country, with its own publication and collecting clubs. As card manufacture became more sophisticated the cards were produced with adhesive backs and were designed to be stuck into special albums produced for each set.

One set of cards that is constantly referred to is the famous Pinnace collection, produced by Geoffrey Phillips Ltd. These are minature (45x35mm) black and white photographs and regularly appear in club histories and 'who's who' style books. There were actually 2,462 different cards issued to cover all the major players (football and rugby) of the mid 1920s and it is virtually impossible to collect the full set. By sending off 25 of these cards you would be sent a cabinet-sized picture of a cricketer or footballer of your choice, and by sending 100 small cards you could exchange them for a large team photo. These are extremely rare.

One unusual 'card' is the Phillip's BDV silk that shows football club colours. These were produced in 1920 and came in two sizes, a small (68x48mm) and a large (150x100mm), showing the same picture of a player in the club colours of white shirts, black shorts

and black socks with two white bands at the top.

There are 19 different Derby County Pinnace cards, featuring such players as J. Lyons, H. Storer, A. Ritchie and G. Thornewell (actually spelt incorrectly as Thornewall).

Other cards of the time include:

Ardath Famous Footballers 1934, S. Crooks and T. Cooper;

Wills Association Footballers 1935, J. Barker;

Ogdens Football Caricatures 1935, H. Gallagher;

Players Football Caricatures by RIP 1926, H. Bedford;

Gallagher Footballers in Action 1927, T. Cooper;

Churchmans Association Footballers Series One 1938, J. Nicholas;

Gallacher Arsenal v Derby action card.

DERBY COUNTY F.C.

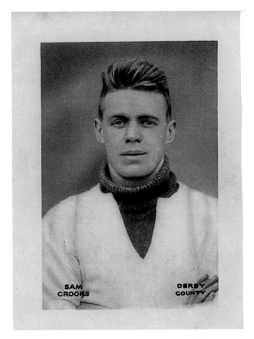

JACK BARKER.
Derby County F.C.

TOPICAL TIMES

J. NICHOLAS.
Derby County F.C.

TOPICAL TIMES

Shermans produced a set of team cards called 'Searchlight on Famous Teams' in 1938, which is quite common, and a year earlier a set called 'Searchlight on Famous Players' came out, featuring Jack Barker and Sammy Crooks, although this set is rarer than the teams. The reverse of the cards had a brief history of the club on the 1938 set and player biography on the 1937 set.

Throughout the 1930s the *Topical Times* sports magazine was published each Friday by D.C. Thompson and was the most popular sports publication of its time and often had a photo card of one of the top players on the front cover. There are black and white cards which are quite large (250x90mm), known as 'panel portraits' and also a later 1936 series that were the same size, but coloured. The black and white series featured Keen, Barker, Boulton and Bowers and the coloured Nicholas card. These large cards are quite common and probably the cheapest item a collector, young or old, can find from the pre-war era.

There was a smaller series of cards (120x45mm) in the 1938–39 'Stars of Today' series, which featured James Hagan (later to become coach/manager of Benfica when Derby played them in the European Cup in 1972).

Autographs

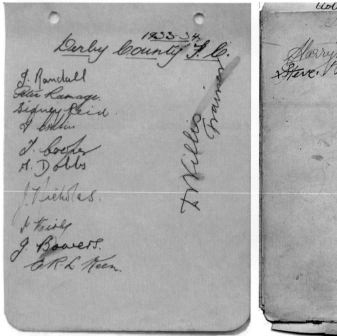

Autograph hunting is a very popular area of collecting and really started in the 1930s when football's popularity was at an all-time high. Collecting autographs was relatively easy as the players often travelled to matches on public transport and could be caught by the autograph hunters outside the football ground before or after a game, with players only too willing to stop and sign. It became a favourite pastime, mainly for schoolboys, and their autographs were kept in autograph books and, for the most part, signatures from this period are in pencil, which over time may have rubbed off.

These books are relatively small, designed to fit into a schoolboy's trouser pocket, and are often unearthed during house clearances or inherited from one generation to the next, and are then often broken up to sell individual pages that contain the autographs of a particular team.

It is unusual for any other items, with the exception of match programmes, to be autographed, as press photographs were not generally available to be purchased by the public and there was no concept of a club shop selling items that could be signed. Anything other than programmes and autograph books should be viewed with suspicion, and unless documentary evidence can be produced to verify the item a buyer should take pains to check that the autograph is genuine and that the item bearing the signature is contemporary with the player and not a modern computer-generated or enhanced production.

During this period Steve Bloomer was employed by Derby County as part of the groundstaff and it is always possible that an autographed page will bear his signature, multiplying the value of the page many times over as it is so rare and comes from one of the most famous footballers ever.

  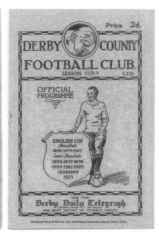

Programmes

Derby's home programmes from the 1920–1940 period are quite scarce compared to other clubs, with very few surviving examples from before 1925. The same style cover was used for most of the 1920s, with just the season being changed on the cover, but they were issued on a variety of different coloured paper, including light green, blue and orange. There was no mention on the cover of the date or opponents until the 1930s.

As these programmes are in short supply, many programme collectors use the end of World War

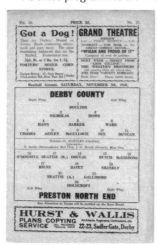  

Two as the starting point for their collection. High prices due to the relative rarity of the items deter the majority of collectors from buying them from this period.

Information regarding friendly matches, tours and postponements is also very sketchy and incomplete and so a definitive list of available programmes to collect cannot be produced with any accuracy. One foreign match programme is that for a match between Derby and West Ham United, played at the Ajax stadium in Amsterdam (see page 41). This game took place on 24 May 1925 and the eight-page programme had the teams in the middle. Looking through the Derby team, as printed, a number of reserves were included who did not play many games during the previous season: Bromage, Haley and Tootle.

The example, top left, is from the home game against Liverpool, played on 9 April 1921, although no mention is made on the cover of the fixture or season. The price of the programme is two pence for the 12 pages. Inside the team line-ups are on the middle pages, and, although players did not wear numbers on their shirts, the programme has numbers against each player, 1 to 11 for the home team and 12 to 22 for the away team, with any late alterations being notified by number on a board sent round the ground.

Another example is for the Derby War Memorial Fund, played on 18 April 1923, when Steve Bloomer's 'Old International' team played the current Derby team. Inside, the player profiles are of the 'Old Internationals', known as Steve's Pals, including many former Derby players such as Maskrey, Morris, Barbour, Leonard and Bloomer himself.

The 1930s programmes had the team line-ups on the front cover as well as the fixture information, with the players numbered 1–22.

The 1935–36 programme cost 2d and had a volume and issue number on the top of the front cover, this season being Volume 6.

Away programmes, particularly from clubs based in London (Tottenham, Arsenal and Chelsea), seem to be much easier to obtain than any home programme.

Player contract

A genuine player contract dating from the 1920s is quite an unusual item, and although one would think they are rare they do seem to appear for sale quite regularly. These are unique to a particular player and one assumes that it is the player's relatives that have sold the contract to a dealer or auction. For the most part these are pre-printed documents and the particulars of the player, his

address and his wage structure have been completed in pen. The contract has been signed both by the player and by the club secretary. In terms of content, the contracts issued to the players of today are very similar, although the wages and bonuses bear no relation to each other.

The example shown is from Freddie Jessop, then living at 35 Powell Street, Derby, and is for the year from May 1936 to May 1937. His basic wage was £6 per week (Bloomer was paid £5 some 37 years earlier) with additional payments of £1 per week when playing for the reserves and £2 per week when in the first team. The contract is signed by the Secretary, W.S. Moore, and also the player.

Photos

The popularity of football was at its peak and newspapers required photographs of the players to print. These were often done during the pre-season time, and were of both individual players and

team groups. They were rarely available to the public, and are only generally released from photographic agencies and newspapers as they clear out old photographs or cease trading. These older photographs are usually printed on thick paper or cards, with the photographic agency's name printed on the back. Some had the player's name superimposed down the side of the photo, as seen with Kirby.

The team photo shows the team that played at Bury on 3 March 1923, and the team are wearing the striped kit. Back row (left to right): McIntyre, Ritchie, Olney, Thoms, Crilly, Plackett; front row: Thornewell, Lyons, Galloway, Moore and Murphy.

Club kit

Derby's kit in this period mainly consisted of the white shirts and black shorts that had been settled upon during the early days of the club. The cigarette cards and silks of the period give accurate pictures and evidence of this.

There are two common photographs that show the Derby team wearing striped shirts. These photographs show the team at Bury (1922–23) and in a second match at Manchester United (1924–25). In 1924 the Football Association introduced a new law that meant the away team would change their kit where a clash of colours occurred. Until this point it was the home team that would have been forced to change kit – possibly explaining why some photos of Derby show them wearing striped shirts during home games.

Club badge

Until 1924, Derby did not have a formal badge displayed on the shirts, but for two seasons they wore a badge that was presented to them by the Supporters' Club: a shield, split into three sections, one with the county badge of a rose and crown, one with the buck in the park badge for the Derby Borough and the third with a ram's head viewed face to the front, as used by a local army regiment. Any sort of club badge or logo then disappeared until after the FA Cup Final in 1946, when a new design was unveiled and worn on the shirts.

The Supporters' Club also issued an enamel badge (as shown) that also dates from around 1924 with the same three images, although the ram's head and borough logo have swapped position. This enamel badge, made by the famous badge makers Fattorini & Sons of Bradford, is in black with gold lettering, is extremely rare and shows the only clear representation of the club's first badge, as team photographs of the period do not clearly show the badge. The ram's head in this format has made several appearances since on other badges, tie clips and pennants (see the 1970s/2000s).

By the 1934 Jubilee, a redesigned logo was used that has the shield shape and three segments that was to stay the same until the late 1960s. The segments contain a rams head, in the familiar bottom part, and a rose and crown in the two other parts (see the Jubilee Supper card for logo).

Stadium

From the time that Derby took occupation of the Baseball Ground on a full-time basis in 1895, it had remained largely unaltered, as Ley's were still the owners of the site. With Derby experiencing on-field success, the facilities for officials, players and spectators were in need of an upgrade. The club

decided to purchase the stadium and adjacent land from Ley's. They could then set about building modern stands and dressing rooms. The sale was concluded on 9 March 1925 for £10,400 for the four-acre site.

The details of the indenture document make interesting reading as they stipulate that various retaining walls to be built around the ground. Ley's would pay £300 towards the cost (the area of land was once known as Dairy House Farm) and the Ley's company and employees would still be able to use the Institute building that originally contained the dressing rooms.

By 1926 redevelopment of the stadium had begun, with the main stand, known as the ABC Stand, being built and the changing rooms moved away from the Osmaston End, where they were originally housed in the building called the Institute. 1933 saw the building of the Osmaston End stand and two years later a similar structure was built at the Normanton End of the now completed stadium.

The postcard shows an aerial view of the Ley's manufacturing site and also of the Baseball Ground site. As there are no stands at either end of the ground and no main stand, we can determine that the picture dates from before 1926.

This postcard is quite rare and collectors of football stadia postcards from all over Europe are keen to purchase

examples such as this. It is believed that this picture was used by the German Luftwaffe during World War Two to pinpoint their position over Derby prior to bombing Rolls-Royce and other targets.

The Baseball Ground was sold to the Walbrook Group for redevelopment in May 2003, and prior to that a number of fixtures and fittings were sold to supporters. Among those items were 20 original W.T.

Ellison turnstiles. These cast-iron turnstiles would have been installed at the ground as the new stands were constructed in the 1920s and 1930s. Ellison's, of Salford, were the country's leading manufacturer of turnstiles and had installed 200 at Wembley Stadium for its opening in 1923 and others at Aston Villa, Newcastle and Liverpool during the previous 30 years.

Within each turnstile, behind a brass metal plate was a brass counter mechanism that was used to record the number of people entering via that turnstile for any particular game. By adding the numbers from all the turnstiles together the attendance could be easily calculated.

Twenty of these turnstiles were sold, some with the counters in place, and each was issued with a certificate of authenticity to verify that they were official products.

The only original bricks from the stadium were those from the oldest remaining part, which was the ABC Stand along Shaftesbury

Crescent. No bricks were officially made available for sale by the football club, although the demolition company allowed interested supporters to take away souvenirs during the process. Without documentary evidence, a Baseball Ground brick looks very much like any other brick from the 1920s and one should be careful if offered any to buy.

The original Vulcan Street sign that was attached to the Normanton End Stand was reclaimed and has been professionally restored.

Ceramics

This Art Deco-style teapot dates from the 1930s and has 'Derby County' painted on the base in black paint. It was made by the famous novelty teapot makers, Sadler's, of Burslem in Staffordshire. This was one of a series of similar teapots produced for different clubs. The handle is actually a player in the Derby kit of the time, the FA Cup trophy is the top of the lid and a whistle is the spout, while the remainder is the shape of an old-fashioned football.

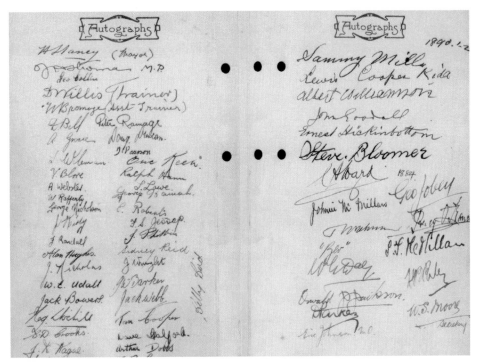

1934 Jubilee

The Jubilee Anniversary of the club fell in 1934 and events were held to mark the occasion. The celebration was marked by the *Derbyshire Advertiser* producing a special supplement in early October 1934.

There was a supper to celebrate the jubilee, held at the Drill Hall on 1 October 1934, for which the menu card is shown. This card has been signed by all of the players and management of the day and also by many of the famous players who had played for the club up until 1934, including some of those who played during the first few seasons of League football (Lewis Cooper, Sammy Mills, Albert Williamson, and Ernest Hickinbottom) and of course Steve Bloomer and John Goodall.

The following day a 'Boy's Tea and Entertainment' was held at the same venue, entrance ticket shown.

The Loving Cup

The Loving Cup was made by famous potters Spode-Copeland and was presented to First Division

clubs to commemorate the Coronation of King George VI and Queen Elizabeth in May 1937. The President of Stoke City, Sir Francis Joseph, commissioned the piece and this one is numbered 16 out of a limited edition of just 30, of which only four are known to exist. There is a tradition that the directors should toast the reigning monarch and drink from the cup.

Trawler

In 1933 a trawler bearing the name *Derby County* was built at Smiths Dock, Middlesbrough, for Consolidated Fisheries Limited at a cost of £19,864, with a displacement of 399 tons and officially numbered GY514. Landing her first catch on 13 September 1933, she marketed 1,250 boxes with a sales value of £1,086. August 1939 saw the ship sold to the Admiralty for £22,518 and converted to an anti-submarine vessel, numbered FY171.

At the end of the war the ship returned to being a fishing boat and was re-registered as GY194 before eventually being scrapped in Belgium in February 1964 with no known surviving items, other than a few photographs.

Tom Cooper

Tom Cooper arrived at Derby from Port Vale and was a stylish full-back who later went on to play for Liverpool. 'Snowy', as he was known, has the honour of being one of the few Derby players to

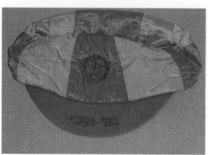

captain England (four times) and won a total of 15 caps. During this time, Derby competed in the Derbyshire Senior Challenge Cup and were victorious in 1934, and Cooper was part of that team and awarded a medal.

Car park ticket

The narrow streets around the Baseball Ground meant that parking was an issue even before the war and car park passes were issued to allow parking in designated areas. This one allows parking in a Prices Street car park at a cost of 7 shillings and sixpence for the aborted 1939–40 season.

Magazines

A large number of magazines were being published in the 1930s, many aimed at the football supporter, and these featured Derby County players and managers regularly.

The *Sports Budget* magazine (The Paper for Every Football Follower) from December 1938 shows the Rams captain, Jack Barker, leading out the team.

The *Football Weekly* magazine dates from October 1936 and was a mixture of factual articles and stories. Steve Bloomer was a regular tipster for the forthcoming matches, and in this issue the Derby manager, George Jobey, gives an interview about his methods and a story of how Jack Bowers and Jack Barker were signed for a total of £350.

Chapter Three
The 1940s

World War Two put a halt to organised League football, yet many clubs continued to play friendly matches, although Derby chose to close down until Christmas 1942. However, during 1941 a Football Association enquiry had found many financial irregularities relating to illegal bonuses paid to players, and manager Jobey was permanently suspended along with several other officials.

Matches were regionalised and a League format was agreed that split the season into two halves, with Derby playing in the North League. Throughout the war period, 'guest' players were allowed to play in League matches and these players were those that were stationed at nearby army and RAF camps. A prime example was Savage, the Queen of the South goalkeeper. It was during this time that Derby were able to use two of their most famous players, Raich Carter and Peter Doherty. Both players later put in transfer requests to their respective clubs and permanently moved to Derby.

Together with some of Derby's established pre-war players, such as Crooks, Duncan, Stamps and Nicholas, the team of the mid-1940s became one the most attractive and attacking in the country.

The 1944–45 season saw a double-winning team emerge, winning the League (second half) championship and also winning the Midland Cup by beating Aston Villa 9–0 over two legs.

The 1945–46 season was a transitional one for football, with North and South Leagues set up to play 42 matches, before normal League football was resumed. The team that played during this season was a mixture of youngsters, those that had played during the war as guest players and those that were players before the war and who had lost six years of their footballing career.

In 1945–46 the team of Woodley, Howe, Nicholas, Leuty, Stamps, Doherty, Carter and Duncan won the FA Cup. It was a unique season for Derby as it remains the only victory in that particular competition. It is also the only time that the competition has been played on a home and away, two-leg basis.

The 1946–47 season started proper League football again, with the same fixture list that was used in the aborted 1938–39 season. A number of the Cup-winning team had departed: Crooks, Duncan, Doherty (incredibly he only played 15 League games for Derby, scoring seven goals) and Nicholas.

Billy Steel had joined Derby from Morton for a British record transfer fee of £15,000, but he failed to live up to his reputation and never really settled south of the border. He was sold back to Dundee in 1950.

A further semi-final appearance two years later against Manchester United was the last high point for many years to come as the on-field success dried up and the club were destined for hard times.

The seasons of 1947–48 and 1948–49 were the best in the League for many years when Derby finished fourth and third respectively, still some points away from challenging for the championship. The inconsistent League form of the 1949–50 season was to show the warning signs of the difficulties to come. Johnny Morris was signed from Manchester United for a new transfer record of £24,500 in March 1949 and his scoring record with Derby led to him playing for England.

Books

The first post-war book about Derby was issued in 1946, in the 'Let's Talk About' series, Derby County being number one in the set. This 32-page book was full of adverts and only the middle eight pages contained a brief history of the club and past and present players. Tom Morgan, Sports Editor of *The People*, compiled these books and 20 were issued in Series One. Apart from the middle pages, all were identical. There are some obvious gaps in the research that went into the publication, with the record victory and defeat both written as 'not known'.

Bert Mozeley, who played over 300 games for the Rams, wrote *When Football Was Fun*, which was his autobiography. It is filled with many personal photographs of his life not only in England, but also in Canada, where he emigrated to in 1955.

Before the recent demand for club history books, the norm was for famous players to write an autobiography, which tended to be part autobiographical and part instructional. The first post-war book of this type was by Peter Doherty. It was called *Spotlight on Football* and was published in 1947, containing pictures and details relating to the FA Cup run in 1946. In 1948 came a book by Billy Steel called *How to Play Football* and in 1950 came *Constructive Football* by A.H. Fabian, who co-wrote it with Arsenal manager Tom Whittaker.

In the last few years other biographies have been written about some of these players from the 1940s that encompass their whole playing and managerial careers; Raich Carter and Billy Steel are the latest of these.

For the following season a new brochure, *The Rams Rampant at Practice, Preparation and Play*, was published in a landscape format. This includes two pictures of each player (head and shoulders and an action picture) and also a biography, other pictures of the team training and printed autographs.

The first yearbook was produced for the 1948–49 season, having 30 pages and costing two shillings. There was a comment by the chairman and manager and pictures and biographies of the first-team squad, details of the young players and a very brief history of the club and records. The comments by the manager that the club would be relying on the younger members of the squad to fill places in the team was to be one of the issues that saw the team relegated to the Third Division by 1954.

To mark 21 years' service to the club, and his retirement from a playing career that ended in September 1946 against Blackpool, there was a Sammy Crooks Souvenir publication in 1947, with proceeds from the sale (1 shilling) going to the Crooks Testimonial Fund. The single sheet of paper is folded into three separate pages that fold out. Inside there are many pictures of Crooks, the last one showing his representative caps, and a full-page biography of the player.

Programmes

Wartime rationing of paper supplies meant that programmes issued for home matches were basic four-page leaflets until the late 1940s. Football programmes were not seen as collectable items in the 1940s and were not looked after. They were seen almost as consumables and many have writing on them to record team changes or scorers and were folded to fit into coat pockets. There were occasions where waste paper bins were placed outside stadia to collect programmes after matches so they could be recycled.

The Baseball Ground was used for other matches during the war period, including the representative game between the British Army and the Civil Defence in February 1944. Jack Nicholas, a policeman, was playing for the Civil Defence and two pre-war Derby players, Jimmy Hagan and Ronnie Dix, appeared for the British Army, where they had their rank printed next to their name.

The usual wartime and immediate post-war programmes followed a standard pattern that consisted of a four-page issue. The front cover showed details of the fixture, club officials and price (two pence). Page two contained various items of club news and a small piece about the visitors and also had the current appearances and goalscorers for the first and reserve teams. Page three was the line-ups for the fixture and the back cover was filled with fixture lists for the first and reserve teams and the occasional advert.

As post-war conditions improved, the programme doubled in size but cost the same. However, the increase in size did not mean any more reading matter, as it was

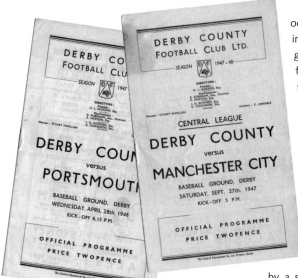

occupied by adverts for local businesses, including the Hilton Arms, run by former goalkeeper Tom Crilly and Sydney Bradley, future chairman. The 1946–47 season saw the introduction of the new club logo on the front of the programme and also on the shirts. One obvious omission in the post-war Derby programmes is pictures, something unheard of in modern production.

By the 1948–49 season, one of programme collectors' favourite programme covers came into use. This cover design, of a ram on a salmon-coloured background, was only used for one season before being replaced by a slightly different one the following year. The main problem with the programmes from this year is that there is no indication of the date or opponents, which means that to identify it one has to open the programme. It is common for programmes from this season to have detached covers and many will have rusty staples. The programme itself increased in price to 3d.

In 1949–50 the salmon colour was dropped and advertising was put on the inside cover. The line-ups took a full page across the middle of the programme and more information was given (League tables and fixture grid), but no written narrative.

There were a number of special issue programmes during this time to mark the end of hostilities (friendly matches at home and abroad).

The pre-season, public friendly matches were generally low-key events with 22 Derby players playing against each other. These fixtures were Whites v Stripes and Whites v Blues during the 1940s. Programmes for these games are very rare as they were generally only a single sheet (printed on one side only and costing 1d), if they were printed at all.

The first post-war home game against foreign opposition was against AC Sparta from Prague, on 9 October 1946. A special card cover held a four-page programme that consisted of player biographies of the visitors, line-ups and their honours and previous results

against British opposition. This also marked the first pirate for a Derby home game, with the four-page programme containing only the line-ups on the inside pages and the back cover having some facts about Sparta. A pirate programme is an unofficial programme that is usually only four pages long and has the word 'souvenir' on the cover. This programme was printed by the well-known pirate producer T. Ross, of Becket House in London.

Foreign tours

After the war Derby, along with many other teams, were invited to play against Continental opposition, and in May 1946 the Rams undertook a tour of Czechoslovakia that took in four matches in and around Prague.

Programmes from any foreign tour match are always rare; during the immediate post-war years it was unlikely that there would have been any travelling support at these matches, so the only programmes to survive would be from the players and officials directly or the odd one from the home country.

There is a badge, of a button type, that was produced in Czechoslovakia at the time of the tour, being black with gold lettering of 'Derby County'. Although one might think that these would be scarce for many of the reasons that programmes are hard to find, there does appear to be regular supply of these badges from that part of Europe and there are a number of possible explanations. They could be more modern remakes of the original, or the original badge could have been made in large quantities. The opening of borders and ease of contact and trade by email and internet auction has brought these to light.

AC Sparta, who Derby played at home and away, presented the club with a large, very heavy, cut-glass crystal vase, which is engraved with the AC Sparta club badge.

Cards

After the end of the war, paper supplies were still restricted and large-scale production was not restarted due to the high material costs. Some of the manufacturers still putting cards into packets

were Carreras, who produced the 'Turf' cards from 1949. These were blue and white in colour and featured three players, Billy Steel, Bert Mozeley and Leon Leuty, in the set of 50. These cards were printed onto the slides in the packets and had to be cut out, so some examples are better cut than others.

There is a modern set of cards, completely anonymous, but expertly drawn, featuring 21 Derby players in different poses. These cards feature many of the 1940s players and, being modern, are in mint condition and can be purchased through many cigarette and trade card dealers. Closer inspection of the drawings shows that some of the player's heads are taken from the 'Underwood' cartoon drawing issued prior to the 1946 Cup Final (see Chapter Four).

Autographs

Football's post-war boom in attendance figures encouraged many more schoolboys to be autograph hunters. Derby had some of the game's finest forwards on its books at the same time – Peter Doherty, Raich Carter, Sammy Crooks, Dally Duncan and Jack Stamps – so the autograph hunters had plenty to choose from.

Winning the FA Cup in the first competiton after the war means that this set of signatures is particularly sought after. However, getting the full team on one piece of paper can often be difficult as that team was soon broken up with the departure of Doherty, Crooks and Duncan in 1946, Nicholas in 1947 and Carter in 1948.

The 1946 Christmas brochure featured a centre page of player pictures with their autographs printed underneath, and these have been reproduced in various publications since then.

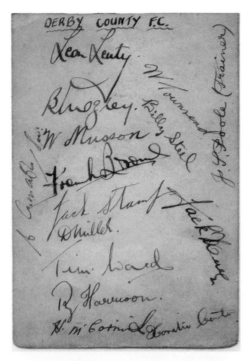

The autographed picture shows Raich Carter in action, and he has signed it as Raich Carter where he would normally sign as Horatio.

The autograph page dates from the 1947–48 season as it has both Billy Steel and Raich (Horatio) Carter's autographs.

Collectors of autographs from this era and any other should be aware that with very little sophisticated equipment autographs can be copied, enhanced and put onto any other picture to create a new photograph. Internet-based auctions are one particular place where these have been sold, and one trick of the trade is to put the autograph in question under glass. If genuine it will generally show through as purple. Obviously, if the autograph is on paper or a photo there would be an indentation on one side and evidence showing on the reverse.

Club kit

The white shirt continued to be worn after the war, but Derby did not play in shirts with the club badge on in the FA Cup Final. However, subsequent official photographs of the Cup Final team show a badge that was to be used for the following 25 years. The badge itself was slightly modified from the Jubilee badge of 1934, with the rose and crown being replaced by the letters DC and FC.

The main playing kit was a basic white shirt with black shorts, and this was changed to a rugby-style shirt by the end of the decade.

The shirt shown is a modern replica, manufactured by the market leaders in this field, TOFFS – The Old Fashioned Football Shirt, and shows the shirt from the 1940s. It has a rugby-style collar, with buttons down to about half-way and the badge was embroidered onto a patch before being sewn onto the shirt.

Season ticket books

Season ticket books were reintroduced after the war and their style and format would become familiar for the next 35 years. They are small books, 9x5cm, that have individual match tickets printed inside containing only a number for a specific game. In that respect there is no difference to the ones in use today, with a number being posted above the turnstile on the day of the game indicating which ticket is required. The only possible reason for doing this and not printing the opponents' name is to avoid large-scale mass production of forged tickets for a particular game.

The season ticket for the 1946–47 season shown is for the 'C' stand (or Pavilion as it was still known) and cost £4 4s for the season. Two years later the same seat cost £5 5s, which is quite an increase and reflected the wages and transfer fees of the players coming into the club. (Billy Steel cost a record £15,000.)

Match tickets

As there were no 'Cup vouchers' included in the season ticket books, everyone had to purchase a ticket for a seat in advance of the game, and one would normally only see tickets for FA Cup matches. The examples shown are for the FA Cup ties against Manchester United and Chesterfield in 1948.

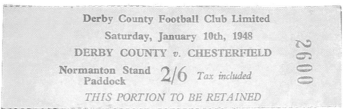

The Chesterfield ticket is for the Normanton Stand Paddock and cost 2s 6d, exactly the same price as the semi-final against Manchester United at Hillsborough later that season (13 March).

You will note that it is the smaller part of the ticket that has been retained by the supporter, the larger part having to be given in at the turnstile upon entry.

Photos

Many press photographs have appeared from this era, both of the teams lining up before matches and of individual players. The photo of Jack Nicholas can be dated to before May 1946, as he is shown with a plain, long-sleeved white shirt and three buttonholes, although he never usually had them done up. Others show Tim Ward and Jack Stamps in the period from 1946–47 onwards as the shirt has a collar and there is the familiar badge on the front.

League and Cup double winners 1944–45

The season of 1944–45 saw the temporary League structure, introduced in 1940, still in place, although some clubs chose to remain dormant and allowed their players to play for other teams. A system of using 'guest' players was encouraged, which allowed players registered to other clubs to appear for another club if he was stationed nearby. This system did lose its credibility by the end of the war, as some clubs preferred to use big-name guest players instead of their own players, and in the 1945 South Cup Final, Chelsea fielded nine players not registered for them.

The League season was split into two parts, called the First and Second Championship, and regionalised into a North and South section. Derby, in the North section, were in a League of 59 other teams and came second to Huddersfield Town in the First Championship and won the Second Championship by four points from Everton.

The League Championship trophy is one of the unique items in the club's trophy cabinet, as it was specially made and engraved for the competiton. As Derby are the only winners of the competition, the trophy is retained.

There was also a Midland Cup competition that saw Derby defeat Northampton Town and Leicester City on their way to a two-leg Final against Aston Villa.

At the Baseball Ground, Peter Doherty scored five goals in a 6–0 win that gave the Cup to Derby after a 3–0 win at Villa Park in the first leg.

The ball used in the Final was given to youngster Eric Hartshorne after the game, who kept and treasured it for many years before he donated it back to the club, where it is now on permanent display.

The trophy itself has not been seen for many years, but a picture of Peter Doherty holding the cup can be found in his book *Spotlight on Football*, published in 1947.

Another photograph shows players Duncan, Nicholas and Crooks holding the Cup at the Baseball Ground.

The programme for the home leg of the final is entitled 'A Championship Souvenir Programme' and is decorated with two Union flags and red, white and blue stripes around the edge. The four-page issue cost two pence and the inside had the team line-ups on one page and a page reporting on club events and a review of a successful season. The Derby team, as printed, still showed four 'guest' players: Grant (Leicester City) in goal, Baxter (Nottingham Forest), Jordan (Doncaster Rovers) and Peter Doherty (Manchester City). The back page shows all the results of the first and second

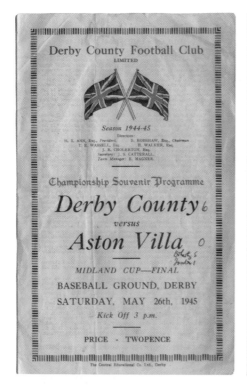

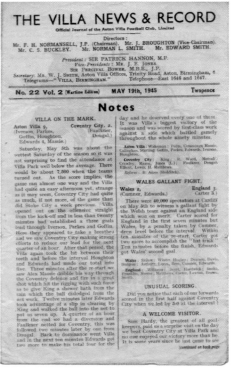

teams in all the various competitions. The second team were also League champions and Cup winners and in their 34 games they scored 151 goals, conceding just 34. This included an 11–1 win against Rolls-Royce and a 10–1 victory against Shelton United.

A similar four-page issue was produced for the first leg of the final on 19 May, costing two pence.

The whole of the text of the programme is taken up with match reports from recent Aston Villa matches and a set of detailed results, line-ups and scorers from the wartime matches played by them. Page two is a full-page advert for the Mitchells & Butlers brewery and the team line-ups are on page three.

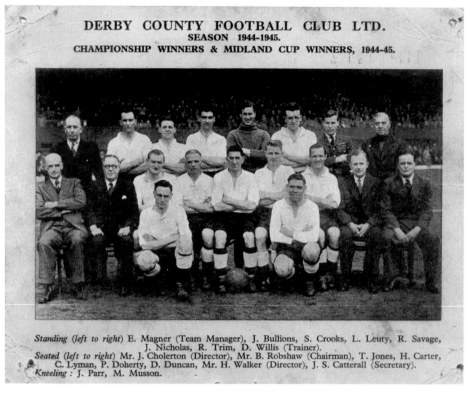

DERBY COUNTY FOOTBALL CLUB LTD.
SEASON 1944-1945.
CHAMPIONSHIP WINNERS & MIDLAND CUP WINNERS, 1944-45.

Standing (left to right) E. Magner (Team Manager), J. Bullions, S. Crooks, L. Leuty, R. Savage, J. Nicholas, R. Trim, D. Willis (Trainer).
Seated (left to right) Mr. J. Cholerton (Director), Mr. B. Robshaw (Chairman), T. Jones, H. Carter, C. Lyman, P. Doherty, D. Duncan, Mr. H. Walker (Director), J. S. Catterall (Secretary).
Kneeling : J. Parr, M. Musson.

The postcard was actually issued prior to the 1946 FA Cup semi-final against Birmingham City and shows the team, management and directors of the Championship winners and Midland cup winners, with R. Trim in his RAF uniform.

Letters

The letter to Bury is dated 13 March 1947 and relates to a cheque for £800 that is enclosed for the Transfer Fee for James McGill, who was signed on the previous day.

On official headed paper and signed by the Secretary, Mr C. Annable, letters such as this are quite rare and collectors who are always looking for something different would happily add such items as these to their files.

A second letter to the Bury chairman, dated 19 June 1947, is a personal plea

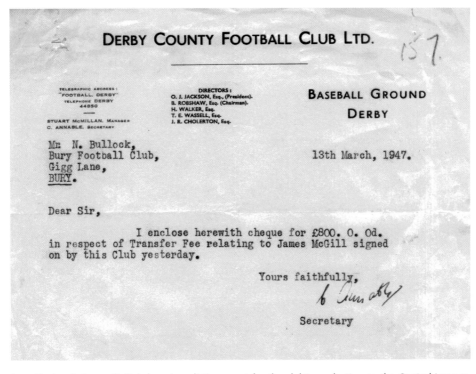

DERBY COUNTY FOOTBALL CLUB LTD.

TELEGRAPHIC ADDRESS :
"FOOTBALL, DERBY"
TELEPHONE DERBY
44850

STUART McMILLAN, Manager
C. ANNABLE, Secretary

DIRECTORS :
O. J. JACKSON, Esq., (President).
B. ROBSHAW, Esq. (Chairman).
H. WALKER, Esq.
T. E. WASSELL, Esq.
J. R. CHOLERTON, Esq.

BASEBALL GROUND
DERBY

Mr. N. Bullock,
Bury Football Club,
Gigg Lane,
BURY.

13th March, 1947.

Dear Sir,

I enclose herewith cheque for £800. 0. 0d.
in respect of Transfer Fee relating to James McGill signed
on by this Club yesterday.

Yours faithfully,

Secretary

from Derby chairman B. Robshaw to solicit support for the club's re-election to the Central League. The reason given for the poor performance is that the younger players have not returned from the armed forces.

Baseball

With the large number of American forces based in this country during the war, sooner or later it was inevitable that the Baseball Ground would attract their attention and a game was arranged.

This was between a Derby County Select and the USAF on 22 July 1944, and the actual baseball has been signed by the players from that day and is stored in the trophy room. It has the players' names, the date and the result written on it. This was the last 'proper' baseball game staged at the Baseball Ground.

Caps

The club has two caps that date from this era, one from Billy Steel, his Scotland v England cap from 12 April 1947, and the other from Raich Carter, for the England v France game played on 3 May 1947, in which he scored in the 77th minute in a 3–0 victory.

Anyone checking the record books will

notice that Billy Steel did not join Derby until the summer of 1947, so the cap on display really has no Derby connection at all.

Fixture cards

Fixture cards have been produced since the very first matches in 1884 (see the Early Years section) and have continued ever since. The first post-war one was in 1946–47 and lists the Board of Directors on the front. The club badge appeared on the fixture card for the first time the following year.

Gateman card

This card was issued to a gateman for the 1945–46 season and confirms his appointment to the position for all first-team matches for that season. He must report for duty 1½ hours prior to kick-off. He is also reminded not to lose the card as it is his only means of admittance for the season.

1945/46

DERBY COUNTY FOOTBALL CLUB LTD.
BASEBALL GROUND, DERBY
———— Telephone 44350 ————

Dear Sir,

You are appointed gateman at all First Team matches. Kindly report to the Ground at least 1¾ hours before the Kick-off.

Do not lose this Card as it will be your only means of admittance throughout the Season.

If unable to attend please notify me AT ONCE.

Yours truly,

C. ANNABLE, Secretary.

This Card must be produced at the Official entrance.

Chapter Four
The 1946
FA Cup Final

The 1946 FA Cup Final, played on 27 April, remains famous for many reasons: it was the first Final after World War Two, it was the only competition played over two legs until the semi-final, it was the first time the ball burst during play and the first time an own goal was scored in the Final. Extra-time was played, and it remains the only time that Derby have won the Cup.

As the only Cup-winning team in Derby's history, there is a constant demand for any items relating to the games played, as well as the various collectables that were available at the time and those that have been produced since. This seems unlikely to stop until the Cup is won again. With Cup Finals, the memorabilia attracts not only collectors from both teams, but also other individuals who collect match tickets, Cup Final programmes and anything related to Wembley Stadium.

As the competition was played over two legs, there were twice as many programmes from the Cup run as in other years, making it harder to collect a full set. In particular, programmes from the away games at Luton Town and Brighton and Hove Albion are scarce. In the years immediately after the end of the war transport was not easy, especially to somewhere like Brighton, and paper was in short supply and was supposed to be recycled. This combination means that few Derby fans would have travelled to the games, and even fewer would have retained their programme, brought it back and ensured its survival for over 60 years.

The quarter-final against Aston Villa at Villa Park saw the first pirate programme issued for a Derby match after the war. They were published by various printers, usually giving untraceable false addresses, hoping to catch out unsuspecting fans on the way to the game. There are many occasions,

even today, where people think they have a genuine programme only to be disappointed when they find out it is not the official version, especially as the price difference between the official and unofficial versions can be measured in hundreds of pounds.

The programmes produced for the home legs of the Cup run were still affected by the wartime paper shortages and were all four pages long, cost two pence, and followed a similar format.

As with all of the programmes, the details of the match were printed on the front cover, the team line-ups were on page three and the back cover carried the fixture list for the current season for the first and reserve teams. That left page two, where any sort of written comment on recent matches and opponents could be made.

The programme for the semi-final against Birmingham City, played at Sheffield, is an unusual format, being one sheet of paper that is folded twice to give a smaller size to carry round. Priced at sixpence, it was quite expensive and the format does not lend itself to being easily looked at during the game. The programme for the replay on the following Wednesday at Maine Road, Manchester, was a simpler four-page publication costing one penny, with the teams on the back cover.

The official programme for the Final has 16 pages, cost sixpence and has a distinctive cover showing one of the famous Wembley towers. Inside there is the 'usual' feel to the Cup Final programme with the Football Association officials introduced on page three, which was replaced in future years by pictures of the members of the royal family that attended to present the trophy. On this occasion the King presented the trophy, but the only mention of his attendance is on the timetable, which details when he will be presented to the two teams. The timetable of events is followed by details on both teams and the line-ups are printed across the middle pages.

A smaller black and white version of the programme was reprinted by Derby and stapled into the match programme for the Charlton Athletic match of the 1994–95 season. This was a poor copy done on shiny paper and was not included in every programme sold.

As with many of the earlier Cup Finals, the FA have sanctioned an official reprint of the programme, and this was done in 1995 to commemorate the 50th anniversary of the Final. A reprint note is printed on the bottom of the back cover.

There are also a number of the unofficial (pirate) programmes for the Final and the common printers of

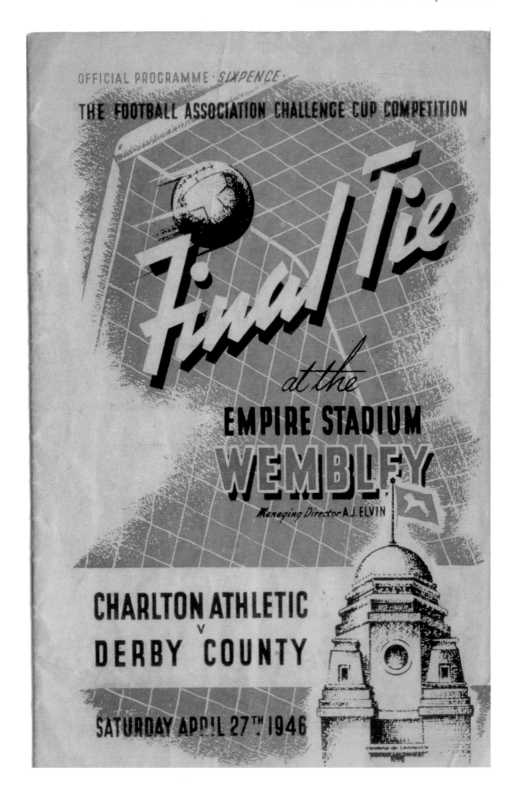

these go by the names of Victor Printing Co. Ltd, T. Ross and Abbott. Most of these programmes were only of four pages with the teams occupying the centre pages and a list of the previous Finals on the back page.

For the Final, the price for a West Standing Enclosure ticket was 3s 6d, while a standing ticket for the semi-final match at Hillsborough cost 2s 6d.

Another piece of printed memorabilia to survive from Wembley Stadium is the dinner menu from the after match meal, which consisted of smoked salmon, chicken casserole and apricot cardinal, followed by coffee. This menu will be rare as very few would have been printed and even fewer would have been taken away from the dinner and survived until today.

Just like today, there were many articles published in the run-up to the Final and a local one was issued by the *Ilkeston Pioneer,* a local publication that opens up to reveal a cartoon drawing of the personalities of the club, as seen by 'Underwood'. This drawing has been reproduced in many of the Derby County books in recent years.

The *Picture Post* magazine dated same day as the Final has Jack Nicholas on the front cover, leading out the Derby team, and inside there is an analysis of the players of both teams. The

conclusion was that Nicholas would be too slow to be able to keep up with Charlton's winger Duffy and this would ultimately win the game for the London team. For a weekly, general knowledge type of magazine there is a surprising level of tactical detail on both teams. Part of the fascination with items of this age is the adverts for the various products for sale in the magazine.

As well as magazines, the national newspapers previewed the match at length and these cuttings can often be found in scrapbooks, giving an interesting overall feel for the Final and its participants. Although not valuable, they are nonetheless interesting.

Many photographs exist of the team during the Cup Final week, staying at their hotel in Harpenden and training at Luton. Others show Jack Parr being presented to the King before the kick-off, Doherty falling under a challenge and about to appeal for a penalty, Bartram saving from Duncan and a Carter shot grazing the bar with the goalkeeper beaten (it is interesting to note that the linesman is nowhere near in line to judge for off-side).

The National Football Museum in Preston has two unusual supporters' items from the Cup Final match, which are typical of the

era – a bell and wooden rattle. The bell used to belong to the caretaker of a girls' school in North London, and he used to take it regularly to Arsenal matches at Highbury. It was then used during the war by wardens to warn people of German air raids and, after the war, a fan called Jack Radford took both items to Derby's Cup matches and ultimately to the Final.

The FA Cup itself has to be handed back for the following year's competition, so the lasting pieces of metal relating to the Final are the medals. Highly prized by the players and treasured by family members, few ever come up for sale. However, the club was lucky enough to secure Raich Carter's medal, which can found in the trophy cabinet,

although not in an original box. The medal itself is not inscribed at all and has no dates on the front of it, as some later medals do.

The FA Cup competition was 100 years old in 1972, and The Football Association produced a scale model of the trophy and presented one to each previous winner as part of the celebrations.

The creation of replica models of the trophy and medals is strictly controlled by the Football Association and to date no replica

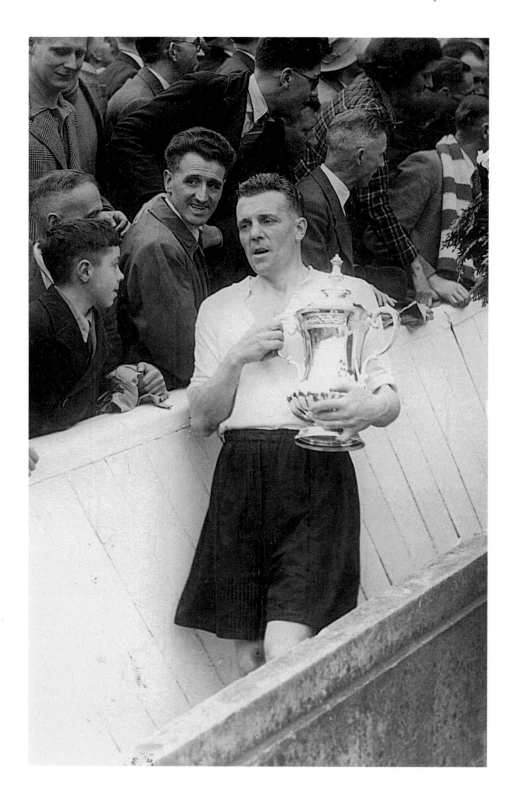

Copyright The National Football Museum

medals have been allowed to be produced, but the trophy has been reproduced as an authorised, solid metal, silver-plated ornament that stands 3½ inches tall and can be purchased with a marble plinth and an engraved plaque with details of the result.

The club issued 'An Autographed Souvenir Brochure' in December 1946, which was a celebration of the FA Cup-winning team. Only 12 pages long, it had individual player pictures as well as team photographs and pictures of the directors and many pictures of the Cup Final itself.

It is interesting to note that the team played the Final in plain white shirts and it was not until some of the official, well-known photographs of the squad with the trophy were produced that the badge was introduced onto the shirt.

A reception was held by the Mayor of Derby and the Town Council at Bemrose School on 6 May.

Royal Crown Derby produced a limited edition plate in the 'Imari' style for each player. The front has the town coat of arms and has 'FA Cup Final Wembley 1946' on the front of the plate. On the back, it has 'Presented to H. Carter by Mayor and Corporation of Derby'.

An unusual photograph shows the gardeners at Osmaston Park, off Nightingale Road, after completing their floral tribute to the cup winners.

The *Derby Evening Telegraph* edition of Monday 29 April had a report that the team would arrive back in Derby at around 7pm on Tuesday and a 'decorated open coach' tour of the town had been arranged. The trophy itself would be on display on the Monday evening as Derby had to play their last away League game of the season at Southampton. On the inside pages there are eight pictures from the Final including three of the goals and others of goalmouth action.

An unusual four-page publication was produced after the Final by Simpsons the Printers, of Derby, and was titled *A Burlesque Broadcast of the Great Cup Final*, and written by Walter Kemp. The origins of this are not known and it is doubtful whether many

Vic Woodley

John Thomas "Jack" Nicholas

James Low "Jim" Bullions

Dave Willis

John Robert "Jack" Howe

Stuart McMillan

Samuel Dickinson "Sammy" Crooks

Reginald Frederick "Reg" Harrison

John David "Jack" Stamps

Peter Dermont Doherty

Walter Urban "Chick" Musson

Leon Harry Leuty

Douglas "Dally" Duncan

Jack Parr

Horatio Stratton "Raich" Carter

of them have survived, as it was not produced before the game, but sometime afterwards.

In 1996 Derby-based cigarette and trade card dealer Mike Heard produced a set of trade cards featuring 15 Derby players and management from the 1946 Final, with a colour drawing on the front and a biography on the reverse. Only 2,000 of each card were printed and these were originally sold at the Ramtique shop, as a framed set, for £55.

Crystal vase

A supporter was so grateful that Derby has at last won the FA Cup that he had a crystal vase engraved. It reads 'A small token of esteem to Jack Nicholas, Captain of Derby County at Wembley, April 27 1946…From a Supporter'.

Chapter Five
The 1950s

Many of the stars of the 1940s teams that had reached the Cup Final and finished third in the League had been sold or retired. Unfortunately, they had not been replaced with adequate new players and the club were to suffer the consequences. A similar fate would repeat itself in the late 1970s under the managership of Tommy Docherty.

During the 1950–51 season Derby had four players who were in the England team: Jack Lee, Bert Mozeley, Tim Ward and Johnny Morris, but four players do not make a club side and the team failed to make any real impact on the Division. With this in mind, the following season saw wholesale changes in the playing staff, with established stars like Tim Ward departing. The new team spent most of the season struggling against relegation, with only Reg Harrison still a regular first-team player, having survived from the 1946 Cup-winners' team. The first three seasons saw a gradual slump, with 11th, 17th and finally bottom-place finishes in Division One, leading to relegation in the 1952–53 season and the departure of Johnny Morris.

Former player Jack Barker had taken over as manager, and for the first time since 1926 Derby kicked-off in Division Two, but things did not improve, with an 18th-place finish, just four points away from relegation. Relegation was only temporarily postponed despite a flurry of transfer activity towards the end of the season, when it was too late to have any effect. In less than nine years they had gone from winning the FA Cup and being rated as one of the best and most attractive teams to watch in the country to being a Third Division outfit.

Another former player, Harry Storer, had been installed as manager by August 1955, and his new squad of players had Derby finishing in second place, which was not good enough to get promotion as the Third Division was regionalised into North and South sections and only the top team in each section would get promotion. No mistake was made the following year, with the team being promoted by winning the League in fine style by four clear points and scoring a club record of 111 goals, with Ray Straw equalling the club record of 37 goals set some years previously by Jack Bowers.

For all this League success, the FA Cup competion turned out to be an embarrassment with non-League opposition knocking them out in the early stages in two successive seasons. After squeezing past Crook Town after a replay, Boston United came to the Baseball Ground with half a team of former Derby players and won 6–1, and is still one of the biggest shocks ever in the competition. Again, the following year New Brighton won 3–1 at the Baseball Ground.

Following their promotion back into Division Two, Derby struggled to make a big impression in the League, but were stable enough to become an established team in that League. It was a hard-working, physical team that Storer had built, but there was never enough money to attract good-quality players to come into the club and make the progress required to challenge for a promotion place. A seventh place in 1958–59 was to be the highest finishing position since the relegation from Division One. 1959–60 brought the thoughts of relegation back into the minds of Rams fans as some poor performances had them in constant trouble.

Success on the field is generally reflected in the number and quality of items of memorabilia available off it. During the 1950s through to the late 1960s Derby's performance was not good and the memorabilia associated with this period in time is, therefore, in short supply.

DERBY COUNTY
INSIDE RIGHT

Cards

'It's a Goal!' was a card game produced by a company called Pepys of Glasgow, where each of the 44 cards depicted a First or Second Division football club, Derby being the inside-right position from the 1950 set. These can be identified as being colour, full-length drawings and the reverse has a red back with cups and flags around the ball.

A second set was published in 1958 with a dull green back to the cards, with a ball going to the left, and a similar front.

Official yearbooks/handbooks

An official handbook was produced by the club for the 1950–51 season. With 46 pages it was really just a book of pictures of the directors, management and players, together with a biography of each player. An unusual picture shows the automatic counting machine used to calculate attendances.

There are early examples of post-war yearbooks, but it was not until the 1957–58 season that the Derby County Supporters' Association produced a yearbook that was published annually until the club began producing its own at the end of the 1960s. These yearbooks followed a similar format throughout the years, containing pen-pictures and profiles of the current playing staff, a team photo in the middle pages, fixture lists and various historical details.

Steam locomotive

There is no obvious connection between the London and North Eastern Railway (LNER) and Derby County Football Club, but the Baseball Bar & Grill has a replica metal nameplate of a steam locomotive named after the club.

The two original nameplates, one on either side of the engine, actually belonged to a Gresley B17 'Sandringham' class steam locomotive that was numbered 2851, although it was renumbered 61651 by British Rail when they took ownership of the train. This locomotive was built in March 1936 and was the fourth of 25 in a series of engines named after football clubs. They were brought in to create an express passenger service down the east coast routes from Ipswich, Colchester and Cambridge into London.

Unfortunately, no known photographs exist of the engine before it went out of service in August 1959 and was scrapped, along with all the other football locomotives, within a period of months. The only pieces to survive are the original nameplates, which are in the hands of private unknown collectors and, according to railwayana auction officials, would fetch a minimum of £35,000 at auction.

Hornby, the model railway manufacturers, produced a limited edition (of 250) 00 gauge replica featuring the *Derby County* engine, but these are extremely hard to get and now only available at auction.

Dawn Covers also produced a postcard featuring the train (with a 5,000 print run) going over the now disused Friargate bridge in Derby, and to mark the 60th anniversary of its manufacture they also

produced a first day cover, dated 1 October 1996, with a special frank mark. The artwork is done by transport artist G.S. Cooper.

Programmes

For the Stoke City match on 30 December 1950, the programme cover has the banner at the top changed from black to a red colour and the price is printed twice, in the ball and again at the bottom. The adverts have been removed, decreasing the programme in size to eight pages, and the review of recent results takes the majority of the inside front cover. The visitors' pen-pictures make their first appearance and the details of the fixture, teams and half-time scoreboard can be found on the middle pages. At the bottom of the page is a warning about pirate programmes circulating, which says that official programme sellers are wearing an official club armband.

The 1951–52 season sees the banner colour return to black and the fixture information finds its way onto the front cover. There are extended match reports, not only of the first team, but also of the reserves, and the only adverts are restricted to the back cover. The middle pages are redesigned to incorporate League tables, half-time scores and current line-ups.

During this season a special Christmas cover was produced, which had a drawing of the Baseball Ground in the middle of a snowstorm. Unfortunately, the fixture information is not printed on these covers.

The 1952–53 season saw the first major redesign of the cover, with the fixture details presented in a box and the club logo in the middle of the page. The programme was increased to 16 pages,

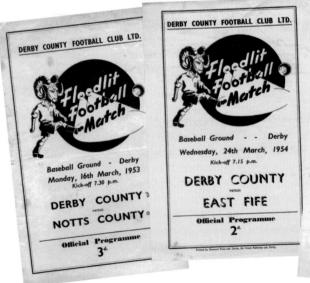

with the three pence price remaining the same. The first photographs now started to appear in the programmes, although not match action, just standard player press photos. The back cover carried an advert for the *Derby Evening Telegraph* that was to remain a constant feature for most of the next 20 years.

Derby's first floodlit match at the Baseball Ground was against Notts County on 16 March 1953, and the programme has a special cover that was to be used for many floodlit matches during the next couple of seasons. The lights consisted of 15 lamps on a crude scaffold frame and there were four of these structures positioned on the corners of the Osmaston and Normanton stands. These were to remain in use, although increased to 30 lamps per frame, until European football came to Derby in 1972 and the rules required that new lights had to be installed.

The 1953–54 programme continued in the same style and format, but had the introduction of the 'Face in the Crowd' picture. It was during this season that a series of friendly matches were arranged against Scottish clubs using the floodlights recently installed at the Baseball Ground. The matches were against St Mirren, East Fife, Hibs, Partick Thistle and Stirling Albion. For these games a four-page programme, costing two pence, was produced and had a special floodlight cover. These programmes rarely come round for sale, so one would expect the prices to reflect their rarity.

As Derby slid down the League into Division Three North, the match programme remained largely the same with very few changes. One such change was the introduction of the Lucky Programme Number in 1957 and the reduction in quality of the paper used to print the programme. There are directors' copies of programmes that have surfaced over the years and these are obvious by their difference to the normal issue. The paper used is a much higher quality and tends to have a glossy finish to it and there is no Lucky Programme Number printed.

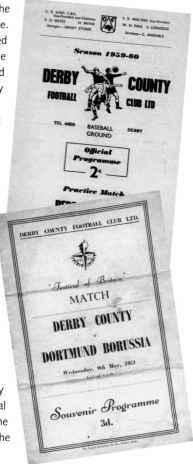

Being in the Third Division for two seasons meant that Derby had to play at some of the less glamorous venues around the country and the programmes from some of these are notoriously hard to find – Barrow, Gateshead, Workington, Rochdale and Accrington Stanley.

This programme is for the first round FA Cup tie played at Crook Town on 19 November 1955, the non-League team getting a replay at Derby. Having scraped past this hurdle Derby crashed out in the next round at home to non-League Boston United.

The pre-season fixture was usually a match played between the first team and reserves with the shirt colours being the name of the teams, in this case Reds v Whites from 1959. The programme, a four-page issue, is similar in style to that of a reserve-team programme issued at the time and it is interesting to note the kick-off time is 7pm on Saturday. Other matches featured Whites v Blues.

As part of the 'Festival of Britain' celebration, Derby entertained Borussia Dortmund on 9 May 1951 and a special edition of the programme was produced, costing 3d for the eight pages. The programme cover has the Festival logo and the inside pages are printed in blue ink. The majority of the programme is taken up by a look at the countries and the leading teams that would be playing in the Festival.

Interestingly, the reserve-team programmes during the early part of the decade were the same size and price as the first-team programme, with no change in the format for the second team. It is worth remembering that the reserve matches took place at the Baseball Ground on Saturday afternoons when the first team were playing away from home, and, with few

travelling supporters, going to the Baseball Ground could have been a weekly trip.

Programmes from friendly matches are always difficult to obtain unless you have been to the game yourself, and the further back in time you go the harder it is to get them. This is made worse when the club goes on foreign tours and examples are hard to find and rarely come up for sale. The tour of Holland in May 1951 started against a Dutch B team at Feyenoord on 23 May, for which game a four-page programme was produced.

Other rare friendlies from the 1950s were away against Aldershot on 18 October 1954, Blau Wit (Holland) on 6 May 1959, where a 16-page programme was printed, and Dundee United on 12 March 1960.

Railway handbills

With no motorways built and cars not as common as they are today, railways were the primary means of public transport. Football Special trains were often run on a Saturday to carry supporters from outlying towns and cities into Derby for the match and also to take Derby supporters to away matches.

The example bill is for the train to the match against Lincoln City at the Baseball Ground on 5 September 1953, which started in Sheffield at 12.05pm and arrived at Derby at 13.55pm. The cost for a return ticket was 5 shillings.

BRITISH RAILWAYS

C1211 (H.D.)

DERBY COUNTY v LINCOLN CITY

AT THE BASEBALL GROUND   Kick-off 3.0 p.m.

FOOTBALL EXCURSION

TO

DERBY

SATURDAY SEPTEMBER 5th

OUTWARD JOURNEY			Return fares third class	RETURN JOURNEY				
		p.m.	s. d.			p.m.	p.m.	p.m.
Sheffield (Midland) ...	dep.	12 5	5/–	Derby (Midland) ...	dep. 6 16	7 42	10 10	
Dore & Totley ...	,,	12 19	5/–	Alfreton and				
Dronfield	,,	12 27	4/6	South Normanton	arr. 7 2	—	—	
Sheepbridge ...	,,	12 33	4/–	Westhouses and				
Chesterfield (Midland) ...	,,	12 39	3/6	Blackwell ...	,, 7 7	—	—	
Clay Cross	,,	12 47	2/9	Doe Hill ...	,, 7 12	—	—	
Doe Hill	,,	12 57	2/9	Clay Cross ...	,, 7 22	8 26	10 51	
Westhouses and Blackwell	,,	1 2	2/6	Chesterfield (Midland)	,, 7 30	8 34	10 59	
Alfreton and				Sheepbridge ...	,, 7 37	8 46	—	
South Normanton	,,	1 8	2/3	Dronfield ...	,, 7 48	8 57	—	
				Dore and Totley ...	,, 7 55	9 5	11 19	
Derby (Midland) ...	arr.	1 55		Sheffield (Midland)	,, 8 3	9 20	11 28	

If the match is cancelled and notice is given to this Region in time to cancel these facilities, the fares paid by intending passengers will be refunded on application

PASSENGERS RETURN ON DAY OF ISSUE ONLY AS SHOWN ABOVE

Tickets can be obtained IN ADVANCE at stations and agencies

Further information will be supplied on application to stations, offices, agencies, or to—
K. A. Kindon, District Passenger Superintendent, Sheffield (Victoria) station (Tel : 25167, Ext. 6)
W. B. Carter, District Commercial Superintendent, Derby (Tel : 2442, Ext. 204),
or C. Dandridge, Commercial Superintendent, Liverpool Street station, London, E.C.2.
(Tel : BIShopsgate 7600)

CONDITIONS OF ISSUE

These tickets are issued subject to the conditions of issue of ordinary tickets where applicable and also to the special conditions as set out in the Bye-Laws, Regulations and Conditions in the published notices

LUGGAGE ALLOWANCES are as set out in these general notices

Children under three years of age, free; three years and under fourteen, half-fares

August 1953

Published by The Railway Executive (Eastern Region)   Printed in Great Britain   Arundel Printing Co. Ltd., Sheffield

Chapter Six
The 1960s

The early part of the 1960s started as the 1950s had ended, with the club averaging 15th place over the first four years of the decade. Bill Curry was signed from Brighton and was the top scorer for those four years.

A new competition had been started during the 1960–61 season called the Football League Cup, which at the time was not fully supported by many of the leading First Division teams. Derby's first game in that competition was an away game at Watford, which was won 5–2.

Tim Ward had replaced Harry Storer as manager during the close season in 1962, but did not make required alterations to the squad until injuries forced him to sign new players. The team struggled to survive that season. The bad winter meant that there were no League games for a number of weeks and the team was too reliant on a Curry-Hutchinson partnership that scored two-thirds of the goals that season.

This lack of goals led to Ward signing Alan Durban from Cardiff City and Gordon Hughes from Newcastle United the following summer and Eddie Thomas a year later. The 1964–65 season saw Durban and Thomas net 22 League goals each, and Derby scored more than any other team in the Division. Durban's skill at bending the ball round a wall from a free-kick was a dangerous weapon.

The 1966–67 season was to prove a turning point in the history of the club. Results were not great, with the team finishing 17th in the League, but Kevin Hector had been signed from Bradford Park Avenue on the recommendation of scout Sammy Crooks. Hector became an instant crowd favourite, scoring on his debut in a 4–3 win against Huddersfield Town. Tim Ward had taken the club as far as he could and a man with new ideas was sought, but, to give Ward his due, some of the players that were to become household names had been brought to the club by him: Hector, Durban, Boulton, Daniel and Webster.

Brian Clough and his assistant Peter Taylor arrived from Hartlepool United and, despite finishing one place lower than the previous year, many new players had were brought in – O'Hare (Sunderland), McFarland (Tranmere), Hinton (Notts Forest), Robson (junior football), Barker (Burton) and Green (Rochdale) – a blend of young players and experience. As these new players were bought during the season, many of them were cup-tied for the League Cup, and their replacements took Derby to their best-ever showing in the competition in a semi-final against Leeds United.

During the following summer Clough somehow persuaded the great Dave Mackay to join Derby from Tottenham Hotspur, and the jigsaw was complete with the experienced Willie Carlin joining early in the season from Sheffield United, joining John McGovern (Hartlepool) and Frank Wignall (Wolves). They went top of the table in late November 1968 and were to remain there. Along the way there were wins against First Division teams Chelsea and Everton in the League Cup, the former being hailed as one of the great nights of football at the Baseball Ground as Derby came from a goal down to batter Chelsea, who eventually capitulated and let in three goals in the last 13 minutes.

Off the field, the first structural change to the Baseball Ground took place during the summer of 1969 when a new stand was built over the top of the Popside terrace, known as the Ley Stand (named after the factory behind that stand), and this brought the capacity up to over 41,000.

It did not take long to reach the maximum when 41,826 squeezed in on 20 September to see

Tottenham Hotspur crushed 5–0 in the First Division. Terry Hennessey became the first £100,000 transfer in February 1970.

Despite finishing fourth in the League and qualifying for a UEFA Cup place, a subsequent FA enquiry found certain administrative errors, and as a result Derby County were given a one-year European ban.

Newspapers

Many of today's tabloid newspapers were originally in the broadsheet format, including *The Sun* and the *Daily Express*. The Saturday morning edition of the *Daily Express* occasionally carried an additional outer colour cover and the Midlands editions of the late 1960s featured Derby players on a number of occasions as they won the Division Two title.

The *Derby Evening Telegraph* also produced a special match edition of the paper that was basically the normal paper with a replaced front cover that previewed each game.

After the match, the usual *Football Special* or *Green 'Un* was printed with all the day's results and up-to-date League tables.

On 19 April the match edition for the Bristol City game was a 'Rams Souvenir Special', with many pictures of the matches throughout the season as well as a preview of the last match against Bristol City.

The 21 April (Monday) edition carried a front-page picture and the lead story is of forged £5 notes being circulated around the pubs of Derby during the celebrations on the Saturday night. The Irongate Tavern had to close its doors at 9.30pm due to the large number of supporters. The players themselves were celebrating at the Midland Hotel, where various speeches were given by the directors, 'a 45 minute epic' by the manager and one from the captain Dave Mackay, who said 'less speeches more dancing'. The match report is hidden on the inside pages.

One week after the last match, another 'Picture Edition' of the paper shows the team in front of the Council House on their open-top tour of the town and has the headline 'Gladitorial Salute as Rams go by'.

Cards

One of the most famous names in trade card production is A. & B.C. Gum, which began issuing bubble gum cards in the mid-1950s. Derby's lowly League position prohibited production of any cards featuring any of the players at that time, but by the mid 1960s a small number had been produced. They started with the 1963 'Make-a-photo' set and featured Parry, Barrowcliffe and Young. The A. & B.C. cards are often referred to as 'yellow back', 'purple back', 'red back' and so on, as the colour of the back of the card was the only way to differentiate between the various sets, with some players' pictures remaining the same from one year to the next.

The 1969 'green back' set featured

Derby County F.C. **BILLY CURRY** Centre Forward

Carlin and Mackay, both pictured at the Millwall away game of the Division Two promotion season, and shows both of them wearing the Millwall away kit (see below for details).

The forerunner to the modern Merlin and Panini sticker collections in the UK was started by a company called FKS Publishing in 1967 and was generally limited to the First Division players. There were 15 players per team and the stickers cost six pence for a packet of seven. They were not really stickers, but coloured pictures that were to be stuck along one edge into an album. The earliest of these Derby 'stickers' was in the 1969 set called 'The Wonderful World of Soccer Stars in Action', which featured some lesser known players from the Derby squad such as John Richardson and Arthur Stewart.

Club kit

The shield badge had been unchanged on the shirts since 1946, but by 1968 the shield shape was dropped from the design to leave just the black ram's head.

The shirts, still white, changed from a 'V' neck at the start of the decade to a plain round neck. By the end of the decade the shirts had a round neck with two black rings around it.

For the often-pictured Millwall away game of 12 April 1969, Derby brought their usual home shirts. This caused a clash with the home team's shirt and so they had to borrow Millwall's red away shirts for the afternoon.

Yearbook

The yearbooks produced by the Supporters' Association followed a similar format throughout the years, containing pen-pictures and profiles of the current playing staff, a team photo in the middle pages, fixture lists and various historical details. The 1969–70 one has a picture on the cover instead of the usual black and white text, and an attempt has been mande to colourise it by adding green for the grass and on the fascia on the stand.

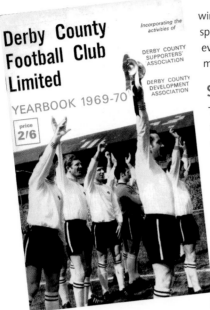

Derby County Football Club Limited
YEARBOOK 1969-70
price 2/6
Incorporating the activities of
DERBY COUNTY SUPPORTERS' ASSOCIATION
DERBY COUNTY DEVELOPMENT ASSOCIATION

To mark the 1968–69 Division Two Championship-winning season the Supporters' Association produced a special 'We are the Champions' edition, which had pages on every player, big matches of the season and match-by-match line-ups.

Subbuteo

The Subbuteo football game was invented in 1947 and was regularly advertised in football magazines and the odd match programme from then onwards.

In the early 1960s Subbuteo started to produce the now legendary three-dimensional 00 scale figures, which continued until the manufacturers ceased production of the Subbuteo range. These new models replaced a cardboard cut-out figure and the scale models were much more attractive to schoolboys of the time and started the boom in Subbuteo. The new editions and accessories

were given the grand title 'Continental Type' and a number of standard, generic kits were produced, with Derby falling under kit 10, plain white shirts and black shorts. All the teams themselves were hand-painted and assembled by a thriving cottage industry staffed by the housewives of Tunbridge Wells.

A special Derby County version of the number-10 kit was available that had the added collar and cuff trim and stripe on the shorts. This set is quite unusual and rare as named teams were not normally produced at this time by the manufacturers, which makes it an obvious special Subbuteo item.

Dave Mackay

Dave Mackay was the inspirational experienced father-figure in a team that was to take the Second Division by storm in the 1968–69 season. The majority of his medals and trophies were sold at a Sotheby's auction in September 2001, some of which were purchased by the club.

Among the items sold was the 9ct gold Division Two Championship medal from 1968–69, which is inscribed 'The Football League Champions, Division 2, 1968–69', and can be seen in the main trophy cabinet. Unsold from the day of the sale was the 'Footballer of the Year' trophy, which was jointly won with Tony Book of Manchester City.

Other items from the Sotheby's auction can be found in the 1970s section.

World Cup

England's victory in the World Cup Final at Wembley Stadium in 1966 was marked by the Football Association producing replicas, although not in solid gold, of the Jules Rimet trophy, one of which was presented to each League club.

The original trophy can no longer be traced, having been stolen in 1983 in Brazil. Brazil had been presented with it after winning the World Cup three times. After the trophy was stolen in London and subsequently recovered by Pickles the dog, the FA (without permission of FIFA) secretly had a bronze replica made of the trophy, which was to be used in public in case it was stolen again. During the celebrations on the pitch after the presentation of the real trophy, the replica was substituted and many of the photographs taken were of the replacement trophy.

Programmes

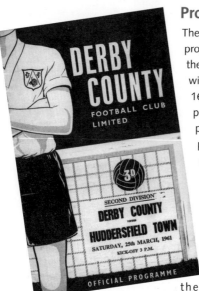

The start of the 1960s saw a redesign of the cover for the programme with a plain, simple and effective cover that shows the team colours and kit with a V-neck shirt. The 16 pages cost 3d. The programme was printed on the usual poor-quality paper and inside the format remained the same as the previous years.

The cover underwent a further change in the 1965–66 season, with just the ram's head being used on the cover, together with the list of the directors. The price had increased by two pence from the previous year, meaning the price had doubled in the first half of the decade. Derby's first home friendly match against English opposition took place on 11 August 1965 against Sheffield United, and the four-page programme is particularly hard to find.

The 1967–68 issue sees an aerial view of the Baseball Ground on the cover along with a smaller ram's head. The aerial view shows how cramped the stadium was, nestled among the terraced houses and Ley's factory before the Ley Stand was built over the top of the Popular Side terracing. There was little

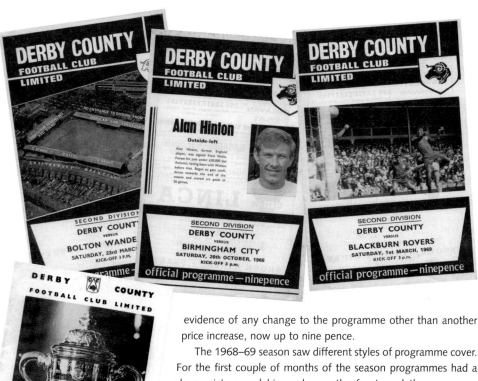

SOUVENIR programme 1s 0d
DERBY COUNTY versus BRISTOL CITY
Saturday 19th April 1969

evidence of any change to the programme other than another price increase, now up to nine pence.

The 1968–69 season saw different styles of programme cover. For the first couple of months of the season programmes had a player picture and biography on the front, and the cover was slightly redesigned to add the full club logo, while in the latter part of the season an action picture from a recent game graced the front.

As the club comfortably won promotion to Division One, the last match of the season saw a special souvenir issue produced that had an extra card cover around the normal match issue, although page one of the inner programme has a picture of Player of the Year Dave Mackay. The special issue shows the Division Two trophy on the front cover and individual player pictures on the back, together with their printed autographs. The cost of this special issue had increased to one shilling.

The close season of 1969 saw the Ley Stand built over the Popular Side terracing, and for the pre-season friendly game against Werder Bremen the programme has Les Green imposed on top of an artist's impression of the new stand. The old favourite logo and Championship trophy appear in opposite corners, but at the end of the decade the programme had changed little for many years and was in need of an overhaul to bring it into line with some of the productions around the country. The 16 pages cost one shilling. After a few games, the cover was changed to

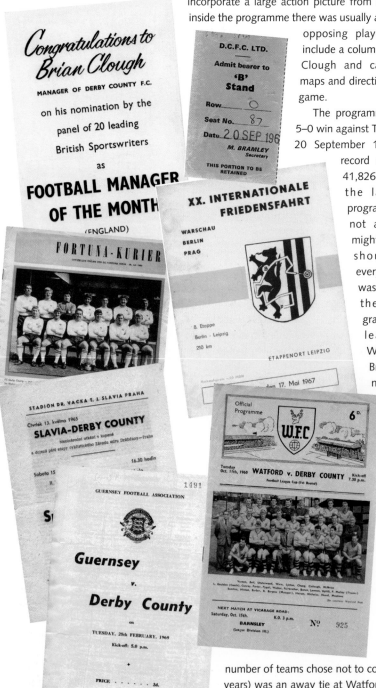

incorporate a large action picture from a recent game, while inside the programme there was usually a picture of one of the opposing players. Other changes include a column written by manager Clough and captain Mackay and maps and directions to the next away game.

The programme shown is for the 5–0 win against Tottenham Hotspur on 20 September 1969, when Derby's record attendance figure of 41,826 was set. Because of the large numbers of programmes printed, it is not as valuable as one might think, although it should be part of everyone's collection as it was an historic day for the club. This pro-gramme also included a leaflet from Bell's Whisky congratulating Brian Clough on being named Manager of the Month for August 1969.

Friendly matches took the club to various parts of Europe including Prague (1965), Leipzig (1967), Guernsey and Cologne (1969), and pro-grammes for these matches are rare.

Derby's first appearance in the League Cup com-petition (a large number of teams chose not to compete in the first few years) was an away tie at Watford that was played on 11 October 1960. The programme for this game is increasingly difficult to obtain.

Anglo-French Friendship Cup

This strangely-named Cup was played against French side Association Sportive Biterroise over two-legs, the first leg in Derby on 11 April 1962 and the return in France on 12 May. There is no information on what this competition is or its purpose and the usual match programme was issued.

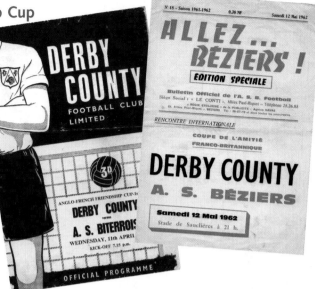

Season tickets

The first season of Brian Clough's era saw £100,000 spent on transfer fees, yet the League season finished with Derby a place worse off than the year before, finishing 18th. Brian Clough sent a letter to all existing season ticket holders expressing his disappointment and telling them what he was going to do in the future. Each of these letters was individually signed by the manager.

The format, shape and size of the season ticket books had remained unchanged since the resumption of football in the 1946–47 season (see 1940s).

The tickets for the 1969–70 season, the first back in the First Division, cost £4 for a Pop side terracing place. The 1969–70 season also marked the opening of the new £150,000 Ley Stand, and the season ticket leaflet indicates that priority would be given to those who purchased a two-year ticket, the cost being £25 for both seasons, whereas a single season 'B' Stand ticket cost £12 10s. Inside the book was a key to the coupon numbers to be used throughout the season, which actually was in alphabetical order i.e. Arsenal – 1 to Wolves – 21. Also included were coupons for admittance to the reserve-team matches, using coupons 26–46.

Clock

The clock that was attached to the middle of the Osmaston Stand at the Baseball Ground was a C273 Synchronous Timepiece erected in 1968 by John Smith & Son, the famous clockmakers from Derby. The diameter of the face is 3½ feet and it is encased in a wooden box with

a perspex (in case anyone with a wayward shot happened to hit it) front. The clock is currently in storage and there is a possibility that it may be re-erected inside Pride Park.

Ramtique

Derby's official club shop and promotions office was located at 55 Osmaston Road and provided a place just out of the city centre where supporters could purchase the scarves, photographs, tankards, rammie banks, badges and other memorabilia, which grew in quantity as the team became more successful.

The number of enamel badges produced during the 1960s began to increase and most of them were for the Supporters' Association and came in a variety of shapes and sizes.

Rammie banks

Rammie banks were introduced in the late 1960s and were moneyboxes in the shape of a ram. Some of these just had the club logo on the side, while others had slogans such as 'For my season ticket' and the seasons.

These were produced regularly for a number of years and managing to collect a full set is quite a task. As these were produced for children and not as ornaments, one would expect that many of them have been damaged or broken and thrown away since then. The modern equivalents are currently being produced by Derby-based Brenda Booth.

Jigsaw

One of the first jigsaws to be produced was a 240-piece puzzle at the end of the decade, featuring match action from the Manchester United home game of 1969–70. The picture could be better, as it shows Roy McFarland's back and Brian Kidd against a background of the main ABC Stand at the Baseball Ground. This puzzle came in a plain brown box, simply labelled 'Derby County 240 piece jigsaw puzzle'.

Pennants

Another 1960s collectable came in the form of pennants, generally triangular, with a hanger cord. These usually carried the club logo and were often issued to commemorate a trophy or event. There are some unusual ones, however, that may have originated outside the UK and can be distinguished by their size and shape.

Chapter Seven
The 1970s

The pre-season of 1970–71 brought football's first sponsored tournament, the Watney Cup. The country's top scoring teams played for the trophy. After wins against Fulham and Sheffield United, Derby beat Manchester United 4–1 in the Final. Unfortunately, this was probably the highlight of a year that saw the team stoop as low as 19th in the table and finish just inside the top 10. With the capture of Colin Todd from Sunderland for a new record fee of £170,000, Dave Mackay was allowed to leave at the end of the season, taking a job as player-manager at Swindon Town.

The next five seasons were to be the best in Derby's history, starting with a Championship win in 1971–72. The team had completed their season and were on holiday in Majorca, while other teams could still overtake Derby in their last games. Having beaten Liverpool 1–0 in the last game of the season, Derby could still be overtaken at the top, but a combination of results left them on top, a point ahead of three other teams. A second sponsored trophy, the Texaco Cup (mainly an Anglo-Scottish competition), was won by defeating Airdrieonians in the Final, the reserves also won the Central League and the average attendance was a record high of over 33,000.

European Cup football followed and memorable victories against Zeljeznicar Sarajevo, Benfica and Spartak Trnava brought a semi-final against Italian giants Juventus. It was a controversial first leg, in which there were allegations of bribery, resulting in a 3–1 defeat and many bookings for trivial offences that meant key players would miss the return game. A Hinton penalty miss in the second leg was the closest Derby came to a goal in a 0–0 draw.

Continuing unrest between chairman Sam Longson and manager Clough eventually caused Clough and Taylor to depart following a 1–0 win at Manchester United in October 1973. Massive protests by fans and players failed to reverse the situation, and Dave Mackay was brought back as manager from Nottingham Forest. The nucleus of the Championship team was still in place, but the loss of Roy McFarland for a year through an injury sustained while playing for England was a blow.

In his place came Peter Daniel, who had been at the club since Tim Ward's time as manager, and together with new signings Francis Lee, Rod Thomas, Bruce Rioch and Henry Newton, a second title was won in 1974–75, this time with the lowest points total for 20 years.

A Charity Shield appearance against West Ham United at Wembley Stadium followed, and a 2–0 win secured another trophy. McFarland and Hector scored the goals and Charlie George made his debut.

The second appearance in Europe came to an abrupt halt with a 5–1 reverse in front of 120,000 people at Real Madrid (after extra-time), with suspension and injured players being blamed. This followed a 4–1 win in the first leg, with a George hat-trick.

Derby progressed to the semi-final of the FA Cup, again without success, as a 2–0 defeat against Manchester United had a huge impact on the club, who won only one more game that season, a 6–2 win at Ipswich on the last day, with Francis Lee scoring twice on his last appearance in football.

A gradual slide in playing fortunes since the semi-final was causing concern and, despite a record-breaking 12–0 win in the UEFA Cup against Ireland's Finn Harps, Dave Mackay was replaced by reserve-team coach Colin Murphy in November 1976.

Less than a year later he too had been replaced by Tommy Docherty (not a favourite among some of the playing staff) and a rapid turnover of players saw the established stars leaving, among them Gemmill, Boulton, Hector, James and Thomas. They were replaced by less able, largely unknown players who were not able to gain the respect of the supporters. A final League position of 19th was not acceptable.

Docherty was allowed to leave to take over at QPR and Colin Addison was asked to pick up the pieces and restore some respectability. Many of Docherty's signings were moved out and it was not until the second half of the 1979–80 season that a settled side began to get some good results. The new attacking pair of Biley and Swindlehurst showed some promise, but the points gap was too large to make up and Derby would start the 1980s in the Second Division. An unforgettable decade saw two League titles, a European Cup and FA Cup semi-finals and Texaco Cup and Watney Cup wins, but also relegation, the sale of star players and falling attendances.

Books

Sparked by on-field success in the late 1960s, driven by Brian Clough and Peter Taylor, Derby's national profile had increased significantly and lead to the first club-oriented hardback book being published in 1970 by Stanley Paul.

Simply called the *Derby County Football Book*, it was written by George Edwards, Sports Reporter for the *Derby Evening Telegraph*. This was followed a year later by the *Derby County Football Book No.2*. Both books were 128 pages long, with many action pictures and a season review and various chapters on players within the team.

The most successful period in the club's history (1967–75) allowed a more detailed account to be written, this time by Gerald Mortimer. His work *Champions Again 1967–1975* was a small size 80-page book. There are two versions of this book, the more common softback and also a hardback edition, which had additional pictures and a larger type font, taking it to 116 pages. The hardback version is extremely difficult to find and most references to Derby County book lists do not recognise it at all.

Stuart Webb and Harry Brown were instrumental in introducing yearbooks in the early 1970s, starting with the *EuroCup Yearbook* for the 1972–73 season, which as you would expect was filled with Championship pictures, articles and statistics. A similar style book was brought out for four successive years (fortunately covering the most successful seasons) before switching to a magazine-style format with many pages of advertising.

As the matchday programme was of a newspaper format for the first Championship season of 1971–72, a special Championship souvenir edition was issued that celebrates the title success. As with many newspapers from this period, many are folded and are difficult to keep in good condition unless stored in one of the official binders. The special issue was 24 pages long, and as you would expect had many pictures of the players and articles about the last matches of the season and views of the future.

Cards/stickers

Trade cards were now well established as a collector's item, and became popular in the playgrounds of many schools. The trade cards typically came in packets of bubble gum from A. & B.C., Topps and others, while the forerunners to the modern stickers were purchased in packets on their own.

As the original photographs for these cards were taken during the pre-season time, any player transfers in the early part of the season meant that the original negative had to be painted, putting the player in the correct colours. Generally these were very poorly done, as the examples showing Don Masson and Derek Hales illustrate.

DERBY COUNTY

VIC
MORELAND
DERBY COUNTY

126 ROD THOMAS

DERBY COUNTY
BOURNE

DAVID NISH

KEVIN HECTOR

MOST CAPS
ROY McFARLAND
(ENGLAND) 26

LEAGUE GOALS
KEVIN HECTOR
140

DERBY
TEAM LEADERS

BIG FEE MAN
GHTON JAMES £300,000

DERBY

STEVE PO

SUN SOCCERCARD No 116

R. McFARLAND (England)

DERBY

International Appearances	1
International Goals	0
League Appearances	111
League Goals	58
Height	5′11″

Alan Hinton
OUTSIDE LEFT

FKS were the only 'sticker' manufacturers of football stickers until the late 1970s when Panini, under the name of Top Sellers, entered the market. For these player pictures, each season a new set was produced along with a new album. Slightly different sticker designs, either on the front or rear, help to identify which set they are (they were not dated in any way). They were available from newsagents and the 1970 set cost 2½p for seven pictures, rising in price to 4p for six pictures by 1975. These also make an extremely good reference for anyone interested in following the development of the playing kits and variations as some of the stickers also show the away kits.

Empty packets from these sets are just as collectable as the pictures and stickers themselves.

Soccer Stars 80 bronze medallions

These unusual medallions were part of a set of 23, one for each team in Division One in 1978–79, and one for the Football League. They were only available by sending away to FKS a quantity of 15 empty sticker packets, plus 50p postage. They are 1½ inches in diameter, and ³⁄₁₆ inch thick of solid bronze. Very few of these medals were produced and even fewer sold, so they are quite rare.

Typhoo cards

Typhoo tea produced black and white pictures as part of their packaging of tea during the early 1960s and these were known as the 'packet' issue. They also produced large coloured cards (10x8in) of various players, known as premium issues. Roy McFarland and John O'Hare were the two Derby players in the premium set of 1973.

Petrol/newspaper giveaways

To try and win the loyalty of customers, various petrol stations started to produce free giveaways by buying so much petrol. For many years they gave away glasses or mugs, but also dealt with football items, one free with every three or four gallons of fuel purchased.

Esso were by far the most prolific of these petrol companies and started in 1970 when they produced the Esso Book of Squelchers, which was a set of 16 small booklets that fitted into a collector's wallet.

Also in 1970 the famous World Cup Squad coins were issued. Although no Derby players were featured at the time, some went on to play for the club: Francis Lee, Henry Newton and Peter Shilton.

The Esso foil badges were also an early 1970s production, with 76 in all to collect, featuring major English, Scottish and Irish teams. These were to be stuck onto a large, unwieldy blue board, and they are very difficult to keep without damaging in some way.

The 1972 Esso collection was produced to mark FA Cup Centenary and one coin was produced for every previous winner, the club badge being on one side and the year and opponents on the reverse. A special gold coloured, larger coin was issued to commemorate the Centenary Final and formed the centrepiece of the set. Complete in the special binder (originally cost 15p), these are a stunning set.

In 1974 the 'Top Team Collection' featured Roy McFarland as part of the set of 22 metal photo discs featuring the most famous players in the UK. These thin metal discs were to be stuck into a special album.

Newspapers were also involved in this loyalty battle, with *The Sun* being the most productive, producing football yearbooks and various trade cards, stamps (known as soccerstamps) and 3D portraits and action cards.

The first card issue was in 1970 when a set and album called the 'Sun Swap Card' was issued and featured three cards showing the team, captain and one other player. At the same time the *Daily Mirror* produced the Mirrorcard set of cards showing a team picture, and the IPC magazine group had their 'My Favourite Soccer Stars' sets that were given away with their boys' magazines *Scorcher*, *Buster* and *Tiger*.

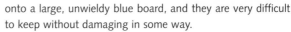

The Sun's 1971–72 set ('Sun Soccerstamp & Encyclopaedia') is probably the most interesting as there were a number of stamps from the set featuring Derby players that were stuck into the special album. The club page featured the club badge, team picture and club captain, and throughout the album there were additional stamps showing other players such as Doherty, Hennessey and Bloomer.

The Sun 3D portraits were postcard-sized and there were four Derby cards in the set: Gemmill, Todd, McFarland and O'Hare. There was just one action card showing Colin Boulton. The portrait cards, although classed as 3D, did not move, but the action card when moved showed a moving image.

After more than 30 years, finding complete sets of these items can be hard and the internet should yield some success, although at a price. Oddments are often stocked by card and cigarette dealers.

Towards the end of the decade, a 1,000-card set known as Soccercards contained a number of Derby players, and this is now a very difficult set to complete. These were coloured cards with drawings of players on some very bright backgrounds and featured Powell, Duncan, Carter, Langan, Middleton, Nish, McFarland and Bloomer.

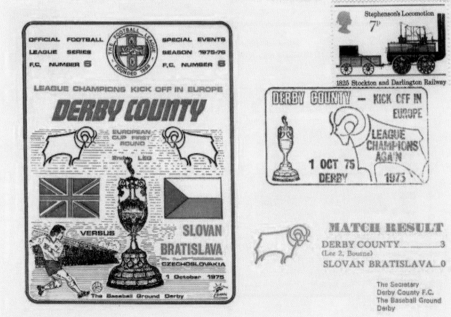

First-day covers

Dawn Covers are the most prolific producers of special commemorative first-day covers for football clubs in the UK and they have produced several that are now quite valuable. The first of these was

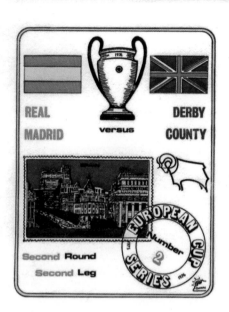

To commemorate the 2nd Round of the EUFA CUP in the Euro Series, this cover has been carried by courier from the U.K. to Spain on board a B.A.C. 1.11 on Flight No. DA.2502 on the 17th October, 1975. Pilot Capt. Atkinson. Returned over same Route on Flight DA.2503, 24th October, 1975. Covers for 2nd Round European Cup were also carried on this flight for the match Derby v Real Madrid but returned at a later date by normal Airmail. Courier C. H. Parsons. Some covers were signed by Pilot. The same cachet has been used on both the UEFA Cup and European Cup.

MATCH RESULTS

DERBY C, _____4   REAL MADRID____1
REAL MADRID ____5   DERBY C._____1

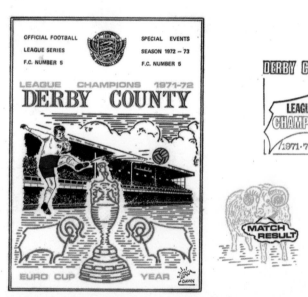

DERBY COUNTY   3
(McFarland)
(Hector)
(McGovern)

BENEFICA   0

The Secretary.
Derby County F.C.
The Baseball Ground,
Derby.

to mark the European Cup tie against Benfica in October 1972, and was advertised in the *Ram* newspaper/programme for sale at 30p. A special frank mark 'Derby County In Europe' was used and the match result was printed on the cover. On the left-hand side the graphic depicts the League

Championship trophy, the Ley stand and a player in club colours. The early covers also had a card insert with a brief history of the club. Similar covers were also produced for European matches against Slovan Bratislava and Real Madrid.

For the away legs in the 1975–76 campaign, special covers were produced that explained the covers were flown out on specific flights, giving details of the pilots' and courier's names. These foreign versions, according to the manufacturers, are very rare. These covers were not only issued for special Derby matches but also when they were the visitors to other teams celebrating an event, an example being that for Hibernian, when Derby were the visitors for the Scottish club's centenary match.

Match tickets

The early part of the decade saw very large attendances, including several over 40,000 at the Baseball Ground, and, with many of the seats sold as season tickets, match tickets on a match-to-match basis were not generally available.

It was common practice for Derby to include Cup vouchers as part of the season-ticket books, and this allowed them to be used for the first four League Cup and FA Cup matches during the season. Only after these were all used did tickets have to be produced for all parts of the ground, terracing and seats.

The early 1970s tickets were produced in such a way that the larger part of the ticket was the part to be given up at the turnstile and the small part retained. As ticket collecting was not a major area of collecting at that time, these would be retained for

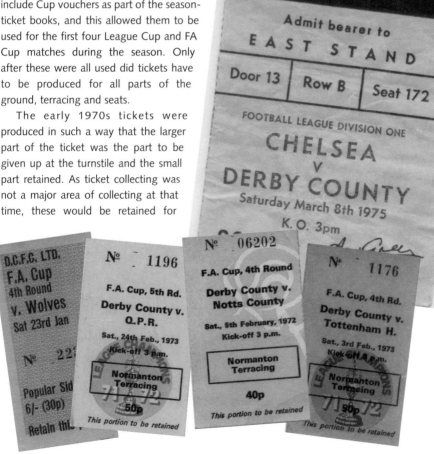

sentimental reasons by fans and they are relatively rare. By the 1974–75 season the ticket had been reversed, so that the larger part with the ground plan on the reverse was the part to be retained.

Tickets for away matches were generally only issued for seats, with terrace places available on a pay-on-the-gate basis, unless the match was likely to be a sell-out.

European football came to the Baseball Ground in the 1970s, on two occasions as champions and twice more in the UEFA Cup. Tickets for the first European campaign in 1972–73 were of the type where the small part was retained and as such are sought after not only by new collectors of Derby County memorabilia, but also by those people that follow the fortunes of English clubs in European competitions. A nice addition to a ticket collection would be the semi-final on 11 April 1973 at Juventus.

The ticket for the UEFA Cup match against Finn Harps in 1976 is particularly rare, as the attendance was the smallest for a European match at the Baseball Ground (13,353). It also marked Derby's record victory in a competitive game (12–0).

Charity Shield

As Champions, Derby were invited to play in the Charity Shield game that marks the start of the new season. They, along with FA Cup-winners Leeds United, declined the invitation in 1972, but did take part in 1975 against West Ham United at Wembley stadium.

The itinerary card shows that the train (the British Rail ticket says to 'Wembley and Back') left

Derby at 8.30am with the match in the afternoon. The evening was to be taken up with a banquet at the London Hilton Hotel, before returning at 1pm on the Sunday afternoon.

Each player in the squad, and manager, a total of 18, was awarded a plaque, which had a silver miniature replica of the Charity Shield attached to a bakelite backboard that is inscribed with details of the fixture. The club purchased the one belonging to manager Dave Mackay.

Awards night

The Derby County Awards Dinners started in 1974, being staged at Bailey's nightclub as an event to make the awards to the player of the year, Supporters' Club branch, supporter of the year and other commercial presentations.

The second Awards Dinner took place on 23 April 1975, on the same evening that Derby became champions for the second time, and as was usual for these events, a programme of the evening was produced for those attending, which detailed the various awards to be presented.

Other interesting items from these events are the ticket and also letters from various personalities who were invited to attend, such as Peter Doherty, who, although he was unable to attend, sent a letter.

European football

Derby had played friendly matches against European teams for many years, but had to wait until 1972 before they could play in European competitions.

There is a whole range of collectables that were available for the travelling supporter at the foreign matches, but may not have appeared relevant or important at the time.

The number of travelling supporters was limited, which in turn meant that the amount of material coming back from these trips was also confined to a small group and whatever they could carry.

The file archives contain many documents relating to the European matches and one can get an appreciation of the amount of detail, preparation, paperwork and communication that has to take place between the clubs, TV and UEFA to stage the match. All the following relate to Derby's first European match against Zeljeznicar Sarajevo from Yugoslavia:

UEFA letter regarding the nationality of the officials

Booking of a local hotel for visiting team

Yugoslavian Embassy request tickets

BBC letter for TV coverage and details of setting up and dismantling equipment

FA letter to confirm names of match officials

Ticket arrangements

UEFA letter confirming their delegate for the match

FA letter giving permission to play the matches

Detailed letter of meals etc for visiting team

Press seat allocation

Expense account of match officials

Football Association receipt for part-payment of match officials' expenses

The away leg had a similar amount of paperwork, with the addition of:

Bow Street Magistrates Court letter relating to Steve Powell, still only 16, being taken out of the country and playing for profit

Travel letter to supporters interested in making the trip, with unconfirmed itinerary

Official Itinerary Card

Tour finance for players, allowed £8 as spending

£3.00   Norm. Stand Upper Tier

Derby County Football Club

Season 75-76

Baseball Ground, Derby   Kick-off 7.30

Wednesday, 22nd October, 1975

EUROPEAN CHAMPIONS CUP   Row   O
2nd ROUND, 1st LEG
REAL MADRID   Seat 116
(SPAIN)

Enter via turnstiles 21, 22 or 23
— to be retained

Nº   44
EUROPEAN CU
Quarter Final—2nd
Derby County
Spartak Trnava
(Czechoslovakia)
Wed., 21st Mar., 1973
Kick-off 7.30 p.m.
Popular Side
VULCAN STREET
60p
This portion to be retained

ROW   SEAT
L   73
EUROPEAN CUP
1st Round (1st leg
Derby County
ZELJEZNICA
(Sarajevo)
Wed., 13th Sept.,
Kick-off 7.30 p.m.
'C' Stand
£1.25
This portion to be re

Nº   939
EUROPEAN CUP
Semi-Final—2nd Leg
Derby County v.
Juventus (Italy)
Wed., 25th April, 1973
Kick-off 7.30 p.m.
Popular Side
VULCAN STREET
£1.00
This portion to be retained

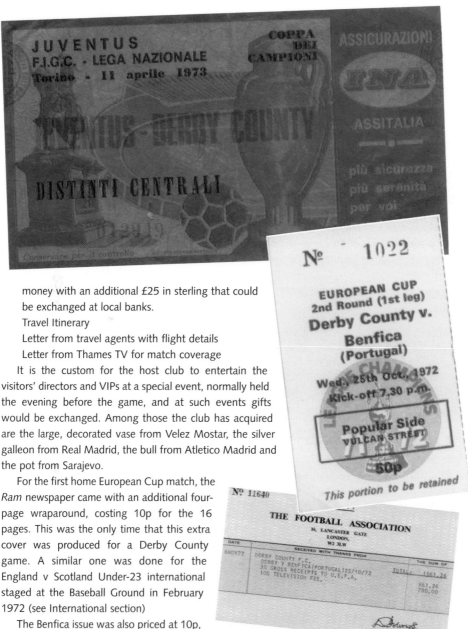

JUVENTUS
F.I.G.C. - LEGA NAZIONALE
Torino - 11 aprile 1973

COPPA
DEI
CAMPIONI

ASSICURAZIONI

ASSITALIA

più sicurezza
più serenità
per voi

DISTINTI CENTRALI

Conservare per il controllo

Nº 1022

EUROPEAN CUP
2nd Round (1st leg)
Derby County v.
Benfica
(Portugal)
Wed., 25th Oct., 1972
Kick-off 7,30 p.m.

Popular Side
VULCAN STREET

50p

This portion to be retained

Nº 11640

THE FOOTBALL ASSOCIATION
16, LANCASTER GATE
LONDON,
W2 3LW

DATE   RECEIVED WITH THANKS FROM
6NOV72   DERBY COUNTY F.C.
         DERBY V BENFICA(PORTUGAL)25/10/73
         3% GROSS RECEIPTS TO U.E.F.A.
         10% TELEVISION FEE.   THE SUM OF
                                        TOTAL   1561.26
                                                861.26
                                                700.00

money with an additional £25 in sterling that could be exchanged at local banks.

Travel Itinerary
Letter from travel agents with flight details
Letter from Thames TV for match coverage

It is the custom for the host club to entertain the visitors' directors and VIPs at a special event, normally held the evening before the game, and at such events gifts would be exchanged. Among those the club has acquired are the large, decorated vase from Velez Mostar, the silver galleon from Real Madrid, the bull from Atletico Madrid and the pot from Sarajevo.

For the first home European Cup match, the *Ram* newspaper came with an additional four-page wraparound, costing 10p for the 16 pages. This was the only time that this extra cover was produced for a Derby County game. A similar one was done for the England v Scotland Under-23 international staged at the Baseball Ground in February 1972 (see International section)

The Benfica issue was also priced at 10p, but the quarter-final and semi-final issues against Spartak Trnava and Juventus were only 7p for the same sized programme. The Juventus issue carries an almost full-page picture of the two captains exchanging pennants before the first leg. As this remains probably the highest profile game in the club's history the programme is keenly sought after.

Equally sought after, for different reasons, is the newspaper from the UEFA Cup tie against Irish League side Finn Harps, played on 15 September 1976. This game saw Derby's highest-ever victory, with a 12–0 scoreline, and for those that collect programmes of historic interest, this is one that they

BRITISH BROADCASTING CORPORATION

KENDAL AVENUE WESTFIELDS ROAD ACTON LONDON W3 ORP

TELEPHONE 01-992 5344 CABLES: BROADCASTS LONDON PS4

TELEGRAMS: BROADCASTS LONDON TELEX   TELEX: 22182

31st August 1972

Reference: 02/OK/Tal/RSB

Derby County F.C.,
Shaftesbury Crescent,
Derby.

Attn: Mr. S. Webb

Dear Sir,

    Propo...
    Proje...
    7342-...

    Our tec...
recent match...

    Two ca...

    One c...

    One...

    Arr...
and they...

    So...
Mr. G...
For co...
On Thu...
on Thu...
Octob...

    Arr...
of...

UNION DES ASSOCIATIONS EUROPÉENNES DE FOOTBALL

UEFA

TÉLÉPHONE 031/44 66 22
ADR. TELEGR.: UEFA BERNE
CASE POSTALE 16, CH - 3000 BERNE 32

BERNE, August 4th, 1972
LAUBEGGSTRASSE 70   SC

    Derby County FC
    Derby

    1st Round of the UEFA Club Competitions - Match officials
    ----

    Dear Sirs,

    We refer to our letter of July 17th and have pleasure in in-
forming you that your matches in the present Round will be
directed by match officials of the following nationality:-

    1st leg at . . Derby . . . . : . .Switzerland. .

    2nd leg at . . Sarajewo . . . : . .Austria. . . .

    The National Association appointing the match officials for
your home match shall inform your National Association in
due time of the names of the referee and of the linesmen.

                      Yours sincerely,

                      UNION DES ASSOCIATIONS
                      EUROPEENNES DE FOOTBALL
                      The General Secretary :

                      Hans Bangerter

Copy for information to the
National Association concerned
    (The F.A., London)

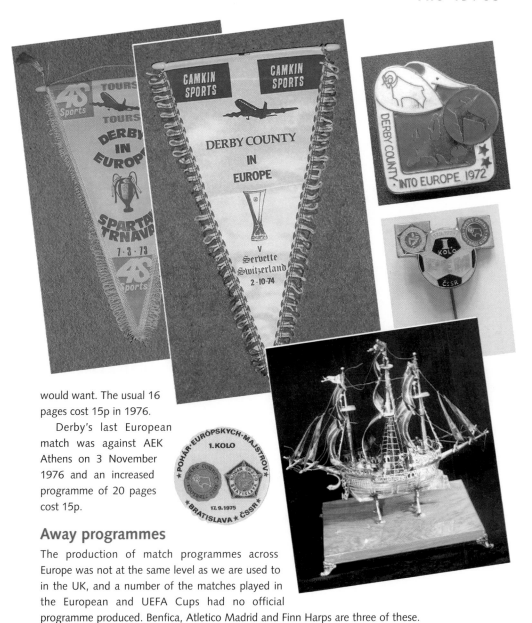

would want. The usual 16 pages cost 15p in 1976.

Derby's last European match was against AEK Athens on 3 November 1976 and an increased programme of 20 pages cost 15p.

Away programmes

The production of match programmes across Europe was not at the same level as we are used to in the UK, and a number of the matches played in the European and UEFA Cups had no official programme produced. Benfica, Atletico Madrid and Finn Harps are three of these.

Probably the rarest of those that were produced was the AEK Athens away programme, which was only available in the VIP areas. The programme from the home leg makes reference to it and suggests that it had to be paid for, the equivalent of 8½ p, for a programme that is little more than a team sheet. It is one of those that few people own and appears on most wants lists. Only one has been seen for sale since that game, which was sold in a postal auction two years ago.

There are various publications available from the Juventus semi-final that range from the local newspapers before and after the game to the official club publications. There was no programme, but an official *Hurra* magazine that was available to club members and VIPs and also *Publi Sport* magazine. There is also an eight-page programme, A4-sized, that was printed in the UK by G. & B.

Litho of London and was flown over prior to the game.

Club kit

The 1971–72 season was memorable for many reasons: the first Champ-ionship win, Texaco Cup win, Central League Title, the new ram logo replacing the old ram's head, the introduction of the *Ram* newspaper replacing the traditional programme and a change of colour in the playing kit from black to blue shorts.

The new logo was created by a Derby company, Product Support (Graphics) Ltd, and took 250 hours of work by the designer and 40 variations before the final image was decided upon.

The plain white shirts and blue shorts were the home kit, with yellow being the change colour for the shirt. Many of the early season photographs of the squad and individual players showed them

wearing the shirt from the previous season with the new shorts, but this is probably because the new shirts were still being manufactured and were not ready in time for the photocall or early season fixtures.

The December 1972 issue of the *Charles Buchan Football Monthly* magazine carries an advert from the Ramtique advertising a replica kit (although Umbro had been producing their 'Umbrosets' since 1970) in various sizes from less than £4 including postage. The kit consisted of a shirt (with embroidered badge), shorts, socks and shirt number. The replica shirts were not as popular as they are today, and there was more demand for tracksuits.

The FA Cup tie against Leeds in 1973 saw both teams playing in their away colours – Derby in all blue and Leeds in all red. This was due to a strange FA Cup rule that applied to that season that stipulated that where a colour clash occurred both teams had to revert to their change kits.

Programmes

Derby started the decade following the style of programme that had become very familiar and predictable. The major difference from the previous season is that a plain cover was used, initially white and then green background colour, with the team line-ups moving to the back page. The Derby programme had not improved as the club had moved into the upper half of the First Division, with nothing more than the basic line-ups, pen-pictures of the opposition and fixture lists being printed. It was generally rated as one of the poorest in the Division. David Moore, a journalist with the *Derby Evening Telegraph*, was appointed as full-time editor of the programme with responsibilities for not only the editorial content, but also the sale distribution and advertising. The new, more readable and pictorial programme saw sales increase by 10 percent on the previous year, but was still some way behind some of the other productions.

One rarity for this season is a postponed match against local rivals Nottingham Forest, due to be played on 30 January 1971, but called off at around midday before the programme sellers were sent out. Very few copies escaped the recycling bins and most of the editorial content was used for the next home programme against Crystal Palace.

Dave Mackay's last match for the club was at the end of the 1970–71 season and a special programme was produced with most of the editorial being taken up with a tribute to his few years at the club.

The start of the 1971–72 season saw a major change in the club's production of the matchday programme with it becoming a radical newspaper format. This format was retained by the club, apart from a few issues at the beginning of the 1979–80 season, until May 1983. The format was so successful that it was copied by a number of other clubs in the lower Leagues such as Plymouth Argyle, Northampton Town and Walsall. The newspaper allowed more editorial than the traditional programme and had a more flexible format. Part of the attraction of the newspaper format was that it was printed and available to buy at newsagents on a Friday prior to the game on a Saturday and was available across the county via the newspaper wholesalers.

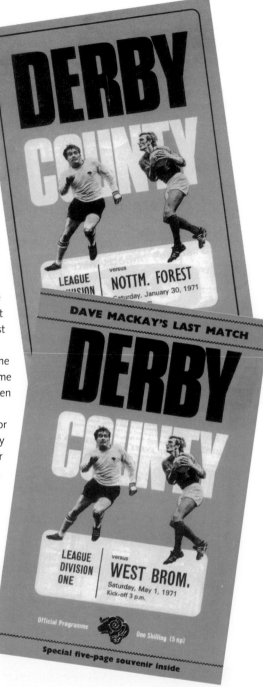

A test issue was given away free at the pre-season friendly against Schalke 04 that had just the outer cover printed, the inside being blank. This issue is relatively scarce as it was just a trailer for the real thing, with little relevant reading matter and no obvious reason for it to be kept.

Issue 1 of the *Ram* newspaper was produced for a game against Manchester United, and as such is one of the more collectable. The front page of this issue states that there were 50,000 copies printed, although one suspects that rather less than that survive, as the Manchester United issue remains harder to purchase than most of the others from that first season. The actual figure sold of that first issue is quoted at 45,000, which was over twice the previous season's average sales, and indeed over 10,000 more than attended the game. Due to the size of these papers, they are notoriously difficult to keep without folding them or damaging the edges. The football club sold special binders for them, with the first one having the season printed on the front in gold lettering with the club name and logo. The binders were a string arrangement and it can be difficult to get the papers slotted in without damaging part of the programme. Being the club's first Championship season, the set is naturally on many supporters' lists of 'must haves' and so will remain in high demand.

With the notorious Baseball Ground pitch giving problems in winter, matches were often postponed, and unlike modern programmes the newspaper/programme was available in the shops on Friday, probably many hours before the match was called off, and in many cases a completely new edition was printed when the game was played again, possibly making a joint issue if there was a game on the Saturday and one the following Wednesday.

A world paper shortage of newsprint meant that only copies that were certain to sell were printed, therefore, some may be more difficult than others to find.

Derby's Eire International mid-field star Gerry Daly with his attractive wife Sheila

The last match of the 1974–75 season v Carlisle United on 26 April 1975 saw a 36-page special edition, also costing 10p. In recent years this has become quite collectable (it was Carlisle's only season in the top Division) and prices for this issue reflect the rarity and importance of the issue to both clubs and their supporters.

By the 1976–77 season the cover was redesigned, not a favourite among collectors, with a mixture of photographs, cartoon and colours (usually red or yellow backgrounds).

A new approach to the newspaper was undertaken for the 1978–79 season, with the outer cover being redesigned so that the team line-ups can be viewed while the programme is folded in half. The cover has a colour picture of a player, usually with his family at home.

At the start of the 1979–80 season the club reverted back to a traditional programme of 36 pages for 25p, of which 16 pages was an included supplement called *Programme Plus*, which covered football, music and motoring in general and was used by a number of clubs in the League. This may have been a contributing factor in the decision to revert back to the newspaper format, in additon to distribution and printing costs. Issue 10 was the last programme. The numbering of issues started again at one for the Norwich home game in December and 12 newspaper pages were printed for the same 25p as the programme. The design had changed and gone back to a front page carrying pictures and text covering various issues. This season also announced the launch of the *Ram Monthly* publication, again a newspaper, issue one being in September 1979. This issue cost 20p for the 20 pages and it continued (sometimes monthly or quarterly) until 1985. The newspaper contained many of the features from the previous seasons and allowed more in-depth interviews and comment, but without the matchday content required for a fixture.

The VIPs and directors were also issued with less cumbersome issues that were basically just the teams. These were generally just a four-page card with the fixture details on the front and the teams on the back, the inside being blank. They would have been issued with the *Football League Review* inside, but it is not important to its value if this is missing. Due to the very limited number that were available, these are uncommon and are rarely available

outside of specialist auctions. After the 1973–74 season these were replaced by the teamsheet (see Carlisle for example).

The last week of the 1974–75 season was eventful, with a 0–0 draw at Leicester that virtually decided the title, Colin Boulton's testimonial match against Stoke City on the Monday, the Annual Awards Night at Bailey's Nightclub on Wednesday, when results elsewhere meant that Derby could not be overtaken, and the last match of the season against Carlisle United (a team that had led the table early on in the season but had been relegated some weeks before the end of the season). For the record, Manchester United, Aston Villa and Norwich City were the promoted teams and Chelsea and Tottenham Hotspur made up the three relegated teams.

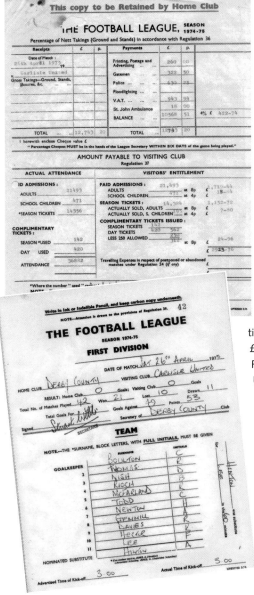

Examples of memorabilia from this last game include the match ticket, a special extended edition of the matchday newspaper/programme, the teamsheet for directors and press and a special match edition of the *Derby Evening Telegraph*.

The official receipts book shows a breakdown of the costs and sales of match tickets with a split to the away team and Football League. Back in the 1970s the away team was given 4 percent of the match receipts and this proved a vital financial lifeline for many smaller teams travelling to play the likes of Arsenal, Liverpool and Manchester United every other week.

In many record books, the attendance for this game is quoted at 38,000 exactly, but it was actually 36,882, with 21,493 adults, 471 children, 14,356 season ticket holders and 562 complimentary/guest tickets. This gave total match receipts of £12,743.20, of which £422.74 went to the Football League and £2,923.76 to Carlisle United as their share.

The *Official Match Record* book, of which one is held for each season for each of the teams (first, reserves and youth), shows the Derby team that was selected, the result, substitutions and the cumulative playing record. The top copy was given to the away side.

In 2001 what claimed to be the original match ball from the game was put up for sale on

Ebay, the internet auction site. It had writing on it to say that it was from the match and was complete with signatures of the full team. It had found its way to Adelaide, South Australia, apparently given to the owner by Archie Gemmill's mother; Gemmill was captain on the day and was presented with the Championship Trophy. While it would be nice to believe it was the actual match ball, one would want some documentary proof that this was the case before making such a purchase and that the signatures were genuine (they would have been done in ball-point pen, which will have faded over time).

The *Football Special* paper printed after the game has a picture of the team on the field prior to kick-off and the details of the televised matches show that Derby's game was to be featured on *Star Soccer* on ITV on Sunday afternoon.

Youth team to Zambia 1975

The youth teams are often invited to play in end-

of-season tours or tournaments and in 1975 they accepted an invitation to play some matches in Malawi and Zambia during April and May. As there would have been few, if any, travelling supporters, the only items to come back would be from members of the tour party.

Colin Chamberlain, a player on the tour, kept all of the documents, invitations, programmes and newspaper clippings from the matches, which make a nice collection.

There are two programmes, one issued by the Zambia Schools FA, for matches played April–May, and the second by Schools FA of Malawi, for matches 2 to 8 May.

The winner of the Peter Stuyvesant Trophy

was decided by goal aggregate over three matches between Zambia Schools and Derby, and the large trophy was won by Derby and sits on display in the trophy cabinet.

TV games

During the 1970s there were a number of TV games that featured football clubs and their players.

One of these, BBC's *Quizball*, was won by Derby during the 1970–71 season. They beat Crystal Palace by four 'goals' to two in the final. The team consisted of three players and a celebrity supporter, and the two teams played a match in the form of a general knowledge quiz on a lighted football pitch. The team could select four easy questions, three medium, two hard or one tough one to try and score a goal. The opposition could opt to take a 'tackle' question and try and win the ball. The team scoring the most goals was the winner. Derby beat Cowdenbeath and Tottenham Hotspur on the way to the final and the players that took part in the competition were Alan Durban, Alan Hinton, Roy McFarland and John O'Hare, with Bob Arnold appearing as the guest supporter. The scorers in the final were Durban (2), Arnold and O'Hare.

Bristol City staged a football-based

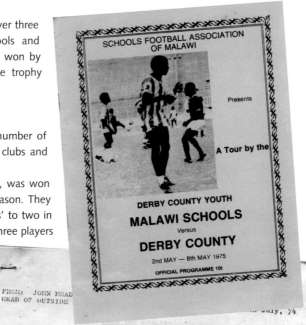

SCHOOLS FOOTBALL ASSOCIATION OF MALAWI

Presents

A Tour by the

DERBY COUNTY YOUTH

MALAWI SCHOOLS

Versus

DERBY COUNTY

2nd MAY — 8th MAY 1975

OFFICIAL PROGRAMME 10t

FROM: JOHN MEAD
HEAD OF OUTSIDE
... July, 74

HTV LIMITED, TELEVISION CENTRE, CARDIFF.

"ALL IN THE GAME"

"All in the Game" has been devised by Alan Dicks of Bristol City A.F.C. and HTV Ltd., in conjunction with ITV's World of Sport team are planning to televise the game.

LOCATION

"All in the Game" will take place at Bristol City's Football Ground at Ashton Gate, Bristol. Rehearsal on Saturday, 27th July at 10.00 a.m. Dress Rehearsal Saturday, 27th from 2.30 - 5.30 p.m. Further rehearsal on Sunday, 28th July from 11.00 a.m. - 1.00 p.m. Record Sunday, 28th July at 3.00 p.m.

"ALL IN THE GAME"

Four first class soccer clubs are involved in the competition. The competition itself will last for approximately thirty three minutes. There will be six games in all. They all involve "Soccer Skill". The games are designed to eliminate body contact between opposing players. Each team will participate in each of the following games.

NUMBER OF PLAYERS IN EACH TEAM - 6 INCLUDING GOALKEEPER.

TEAMS PLAY IN FOLLOWING ORDER.

GAME 1	GAME 2	GAME 3	GAME 4
CHELSEA	WOLVES	DERBY COUNTY	BRISTOL CITY
WOLVES	DERBY COUNTY	BRISTOL CITY	CHELSEA
DERBY COUNTY	BRISTOL CITY	CHELSEA	WOLVES
BRISTOL CITY	CHELSEA	WOLVES	DERBY COUNTY

GAME 5   GAME 6

competition called *All in the Game* that was based on football skills for eight different teams and shown on ITV. Derby beat Norwich City in the final with a team led by Alan Hinton with Colin Murphy as coach and players Carruthers, Chamberlain, Langan, King, O'Riordan and Moseley.

Derby were also regular competitiors in the *Daily Express* five-a-side competition, played indoors at Wembley, and won it once in 1973.

Derby Evening Telegraph pre-match newspaper editions

The *Derby Evening Telegraph* produced a special pre-match version of the newspaper, which was the normal Saturday edition with a different front cover, relating specifically to the match and with the latest probable team line-ups. These were on sale in the town centre and around the ground and, for younger supporters, gave a cheaper alternative to the programme. These papers may have affected programme sales as it is unlikely that people would buy both, unless for a specific special edition.

The paper brings us daily information and comment from the club and normally this is confined to the back pages, but there are exceptional circumstances where the club dominated the front page. On Tuesday 9 May 1972 'Rams Champions!' was the main headline of the day, and this edition also included an eight-page pull out section covering the achievement. The edition of Thursday 24 April 1975 carried the simple headline 'The Champions'.

As well as the pre-match edition, the *Football Special* was produced on a Saturday evening containing the first match report of the Derby game, all the League results from the days' matches and the up-to-date League tables. This started off printed on green paper and, as the cost of newspaper increased, was changed to normal paper and then back to green in recent years. The edition dated 29 March 1975 relates to the Derby v Luton game in which Roger Davies scored all five goals. Interestingly, the League table shows Derby in seventh place with just eight games to play, in a season that the Championship was won for a second time.

Subbuteo sets

The change in playing kit in 1971–72 took a year to be fed through to the Subbuteo manufacturers and by 1972–73 Derby's kit had moved from the number 10

(see 1960s) to a kit 18, also used by Tottenham Hotspur and Bolton Wanderers. The colour of the shorts was clearly the wrong blue for any of those teams and a new number 154 was produced for the 1973–74 season that was more suitable (previously released as the England team for the 1970 World Cup). They remained associated with this kit until 1983.

Badges

Badge collecting became a huge part of sports memorabilia, and on matchdays many traders could be found selling different badges outside the ground. The main badge manufacturers were   Coffer, Reeves and Fattorini, and it was mainly the club that had badges made for them, among other metal items such as cufflinks and tieclips. The early badges made for the Junior Rams are particularly rare and keenly sought after.

Bring back Clough and Taylor campaign

Few people could have forseen the events of a week in mid-October 1973 following a 1–0 victory at Old Trafford on the Saturday. Brian Clough and Peter Taylor resigned from their positions on the Monday, while Derby had four players on England duty (McFarland, Todd, Nish and Hector) with an important qualifying game against Poland to play on the Wednesday evening. Kevin Hector nearly became a national hero as his last-minute effort was scrambled off the line. A strong protest movement was soon started and many thousands demonstrated through the streets of Derby, signing petitions and producing newsletters.

The next League match was against local rivals Leicester City on 20 October and Jimmy Gordon took the role of caretaker-manager. The *Derby Evening Telegraph*'s match edition featured Kevin Hector in England kit and had a number of comments from readers on the back cover, and also details of a writ issued by Clough against the directors.

Brian Clough was also a shareholder, having some 50 shares dated 18 November 1971. In

February 1979 he sold them but could not find his original certificate so had to fill in the indemnity form, finally severing all connection with the club.

Pre-season and tour matches

Derby County had been doing foreign tours as long ago as Steve Bloomer's days and before 1940 there were regular matches against Scottish opposition, but as Champions of England, Derby were bombarded with requests for pre-season friendlies and foreign tour matches and invitations to take part in various tournaments, many of which had to be turned down.

Tours took place to Holland, West Germany, France and Spain and it was usual for the management, staff, players and travelling press to be issued with itinerary cards for the few days that they were away. These cards contain day-by-day details of the tour and matches, the hotel and list of the official travelling party.

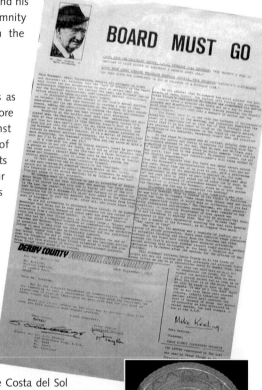

There were various trips to Spain, one being to Malaga where they took part in the Costa del Sol tournament in August 1974. The rare programme for this event is a large brochure style and has 70 pages.

The cancellation of matches, particularly around Christmas time, due to adverse weather conditions or the need for a mid-season break, saw the club play a number of games in the Middle East. The highly decorated silver plate comes from one such game against Zamalek Sporting Club in Cairo, Egypt, for a game played on 15 December 1975.

An exhibition tournament was arranged in Singapore between Derby County, Coventry City and Everton in 1974, called the Anchor Soccer Festival. There is also a programme from this tournament,

but it is extremely unlikely that many will exist in this country.

Other matches saw the team go to Iraq, Qatar and Syria (where war broke out when the team arrived).

In August 1977 they were invited to Belgium to play in a four-team tournament against Queen's Park Rangers, AEK Athens and Club Bruges. The programme cover shows Roger Davies holding a trophy during his time in Belgium.

Other rare away programmes are the single sheet from the friendly match against Paris St Germain played at the end of the 1975–76 season, and a pre-season match against Schalke 04 in Germany as part of the tour of Holland and Germany as the new English Champions.

As Champions of England, there were many offers for pre-season matches, and the club decided to tour Holland and Scotland in July 1975 before returning home for the Charity Shield match. The tour started in Holland with a game against Feyenoord before moving to Scotland for a game against Glasgow Celtic, the only time the two clubs have played each other (despite rumours that a game took place or was arranged in the late 1950s) and then on to Edinburgh to play Hibernian for their centenary match.

Challenge Match

Celtic v Derby County

CELTIC PARK
August 2nd, 1975
Kick-off 3 p.m.
Official Souvenir Programme   10p

Sponsored trophies

The country's first sponsored competition, The Watney Cup, was an invitation only competition and two teams from each division were invited into it.

Watney's wanted the teams to be the highest scoring that were not involved in European competitions. The competition was the first to use the penalty shoot-out as a way of deciding a drawn game after extra-time.

Derby won 5–3 (after extra time) at Fulham in the first round, 1–0 over Sheffield United in the semi-final and 4–1 over Manchester United in the Final at the Baseball Ground.

The usual format of the competition programmes was to have a picture of the trophy on the front cover along with rosettes of the competing clubs. The programmes contained articles of general interest, with the Final edition containing reports of the two semi-final matches. Both Derby's home programmes were 16 pages, costing one shilling.

The trophy for the competition is one of the largest football trophies you will see. Derby were the first winners of the Cup, and Stoke City the last in 1973. Derby borrowed the trophy from Whitbreads Brewery for the 'Rams in Focus'

129
FULHAM FOOTBALL CLUB LIMITED
Craven Cottage, Stevenage Road, Fulham, S.W.6

FIRST ROUND
WATNEY MANN CUP
SATURDAY, 1st AUGUST, 1970
Kick-Off: 3·00 p.m.

Should circumstances, over which we have no control, prevent the match being played as advertised, the tickets sold will be available for the date upon which the match takes place.
NO MONEY WILL BE REFUNDED.

ROW   SEAT
M   7   STAND
15/-   F
This Portion to be Retained

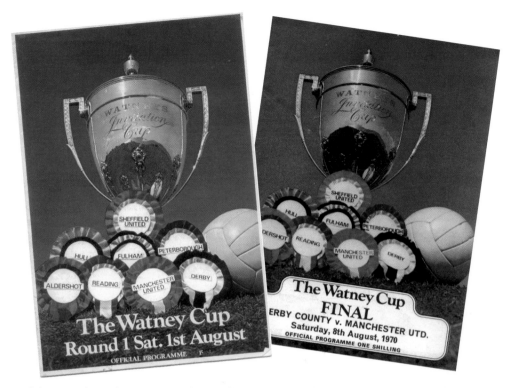

exhibition at the Derby Museum and Art Gallery in 1990 and have been the custodians of it ever since. As well as the large trophy, the club were also presented with a small tankard, the same as those awarded to the players, which they were to keep.

Season tickets

There was no change in the format from the previous seasons, but it is unusual to find a 1970–71 season-ticket book with its front cover intact, as you had to tear it off and send it back if you wanted to renew your ticket for the following season. It is always interesting to note the prices of the tickets – the Normanton Stand cost £10 for the season. Also the key to which coupon would be used at any specific game has been removed.

One suspects that the season-ticket books were printed some time in advance of the new club logo, as the old ram's head is shown on the cover and for the Championship season you were asked to pay £6.20 for a place on the Popular Side terracing.

The new logo is evident on the 1972–73 tickets and a 'C' stand ticket cost £21.

Fixture cards

One of the few free collectables that can be picked up at the start of every season is a fixture card. These have been around for many years and the design changed little over the years (see 1940s and 1950s examples).

The primary aim of these cards is to list the fixtures of the first team and usually reserves in an

easy-to-read format and on a card that would fit into a personal diary or wallet.

The drawings used on the top of the 1972–73 and 1973–74 cards were also used on the front cover of the reserve-team programmes for those years. These cards are 16½ x7½cm wide and the 1975–76 version was changed to a landscape format on the cover, although internally it remained the same.

An extended version (18½cm) was used as the 1979–80 card and it was changed to an all-blue cover.

Testimonials

The 1970s was the most prolific time in Derby's history for player testimonials, a reward for players for 10 years' service to the club or those who had been forced to retire due to injury. It was usual for the directors to allow a match to be played at the Baseball Ground and a special programme for the game would be printed and sometimes also a brochure. While the programme relates to one match, there were often other events held throughout the season for the benefit of the player, such as dinners and golf events.

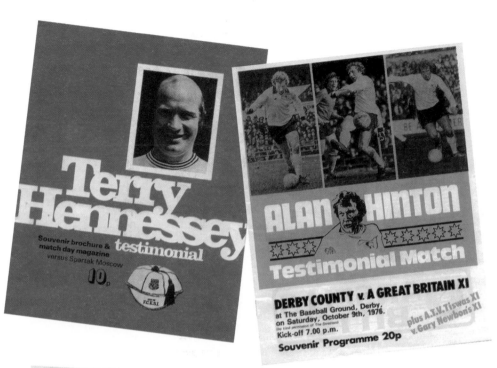

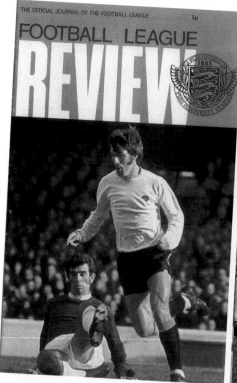

Football League Review

During the late 1960s and 1970–71 season, the *Football League Review* magazine was being inserted into the programmes of many League clubs free of charge, but stocks did run out on occasions as Derby's attendances reached new heights.

Derby players have featured on a number of the covers of these magazines, whose editor was Harry Brown, who became the editor of the *Ram* newspaper and match programme into the 1980s. As well as players appearing on the cover, the magazine printed many colour team pictures.

These *Football League Reviews* have largely been discarded by collectors and dealers over the years as an irrelevant and unnecessary addition. Some clubs at the time were not too keen on the publication because it became the official mouthpiece of the Football League. As a result, large numbers of these have been thrown away, destroyed or recycled, but as the

first issues are nearly 40 years old, they have become quite collectable and can still be purchased from dealers at a very cheap rate.

Baseball Ground

Plans were made early in the 1970s to completely redevelop the Baseball Ground as a fully modern, concrete stadium, starting with the Normanton End. For various reasons, these were never actioned, but other changes around the stadium were being made.

The advent of European football meant that the old floodlights, crudely built on scaffolding on the top of the Normanton and Osmaston stands, had to be replaced by modern lighting that reached the UEFA standard and allowed colour TV cameras to be used for the night matches.

The pitch at Derby had suffered during wet weather for many years as poor drainage around the local streets, still occupied by terraced houses, coupled with the fact that the pitch was below street level, meant postponements were inevitable due to waterlogging. The pitch had become infamous, and when it was playable

Reserved
for the Chairman...
Mr Sam Longson

the mud was ankle deep, and during the latter part of the season became rock hard and covered with sand.

At the end of the 1974–75 Championship season, the decision was made to replace the pitch and install undersoil heating at the same time. A clever piece of marketing saw the centre circle packaged into plastic capsules and sold, with a backing board detailing the famous players who had played on it. In reality this piece of centre circle was a lump of dried mud with no sign of grass, and advertising at the time suggested that 10,000 such pieces were available for sale. The penalty spots were taken by directors and officials of the club, as shown in the publicity photo of chairman Sam Longson taking the Osmaston End penalty spot.

Transfers

There are two documents sent back from the Football Association regarding player transfers, that are held by the club. One is the Transfer Registration document confirming the transfer of Bruce Rioch from Aston Villa in February 1974, and the other is

No. **H** 15651 SEASON 1973 - 74 :

THE FOOTBALL ASSOCIATION

Transfer of a Professional Player

FORM H

I hereby certify that I have this day transferred ___ BRUCE RIOCH ___

from ___ ASTON VILLA ___ Club to ___ DERBY COUNTY ___ Club

21 FEB 1974

Date ___

Secretary of
The Football Association

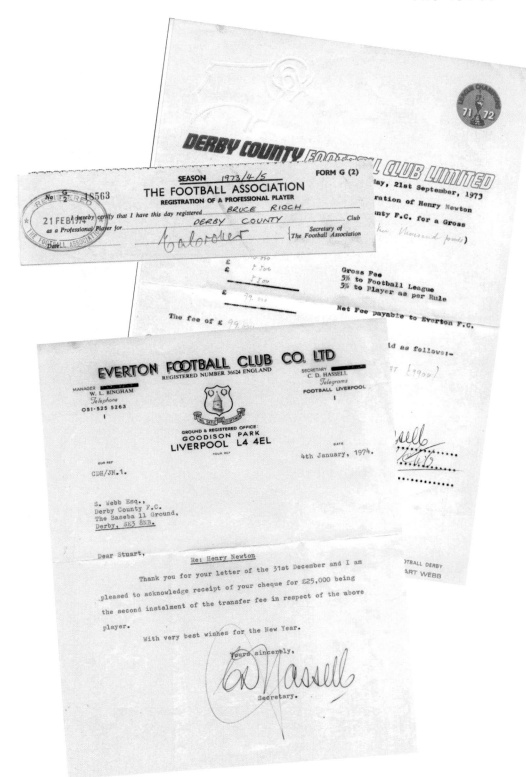

the document of agreement between Derby and Everton, confirming the transfer of Henry Newton in September 1973 for a fee of £110,000, of which five percent went to the Football League and five percent to the player, leaving a balance of £99,000 payable in three installments to Everton. The document is signed by the Everton and Derby club secretaries and also Peter Taylor (whose signature is not often seen). There is also a letter from Everton confirming receipt of a second instalment of £25,000 that was due to be paid by 31 December 1973.

Annual Report and accounts

Looking at the accounts for a few years in the 1970s shows that the proportion of wages to match receipts increased from 44 percent in 1970 to 54 percent in 1976.

The 1970 accounts report that the total wage bill for the year was £136,642, with gate receipts (including the away match receipts) of £308,000. Only one player in the 1969–70 season was earning between £10–12,500.

The Championship season of 1971–72 saw the wage bill rise from £130,000 to £233,000 in one year, with match receipts increasing to £427,500. A noticeable change in the amount the top players were earning was that five players now fell into the £10–£12,500 bracket and the top wage earner was on £20–£22,500. However, there was an overall profit of £87,000 for the year.

After the last European Cup campaign had boosted receipts to £766,500, the wage bill had risen to £334,000 and transfer fees had meant there was an overall loss of £1,129 for the year.

These accounts booklets were only sent to people on the share register as shareholders at the end of the financial year. It is, therefore, unusual for these to be found.

England

The Football Association sent a letter to the club informing them that Roy McFarland and Colin Todd had been selected for the England squad for the Home Internationals and friendly against Argentina in May 1974. There is also the player's version of the letter with the

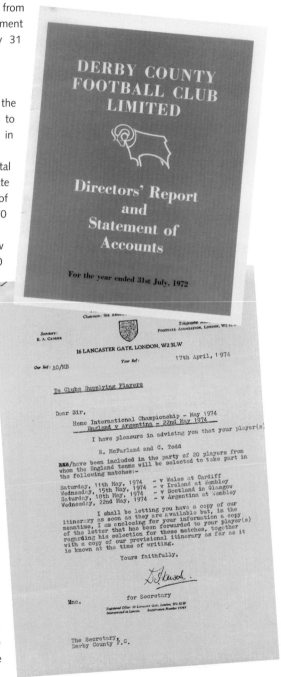

planned itinerary for the matches.

As a result of an Achilles tendon injury sustained in the Northern Ireland match in the Home International, Roy McFarland spent most of the following season (nearly a full calendar year since his last first-team game) recovering, and managed to play in the final four matches of the second Championship season. He was allowed a Championship medal even though he did not meet the criteria of matches played. This was due to him being injured on England duty and consequently missing the majority of the successful season.

The letter from the Royal National Orthopaedic Hospital suggested that it would be at least four months before he would be able to play again. The FA also wrote to the club explaining the nature of the injury and course of treatment. It did spark a great deal of communication between Derby and the FA regarding an insurance claim for losing his services while in the care of the national team.

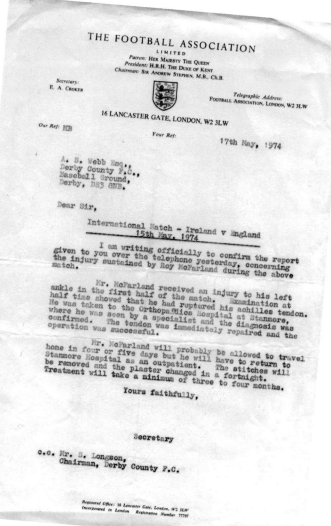

Silk scarves

The 1970s saw the craze of silk scarves and many different designs were produced. Some of the early ones that were originally blue have turned to purple over the years.
Derby – Super Kings, with European logo
Derby County – League Champions
Derby County – The Rams

Derby County on both sides
Derby County – Leicester City Hotel Pontinenal Torremolinos – Europe 1974

Printed autograph sheets

The demand for players' autographs was so great that pre-printed sheets were produced and, instead of just the copied versions from previous years, Derby had them properly printed so that the signatures appear in blue. The example shows the 1972–73 version with the players in formation and the Championship logo at the top of the page.

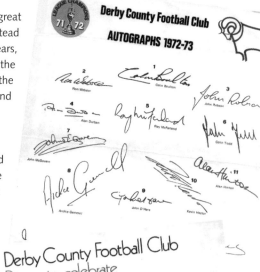

Championship celebrations

The Championship of 1971–72 was celebrated by an Official Reception and Dance given by the Mayor of Derby and the Town Council, held at the Pennine Hotel on 17 May 1972. Inside the programme Steve Powell is listed as an apprentice, although he actually played six games (including the last League game against Liverpool) during the season. The match ball from the Liverpool game was raffled during the evening, according to the menu, although it has not been seen since.

The players returned from their end-of-season stay as Champions and were presented

DERBY COUNTY FOOTBALL CLUB LIMITED

The Chairman, Directors, Management and players thank you most sincerely for your kind message of congratulations to the club on winning the First Division Championship.

The Baseball Ground, Derby.
May 1975

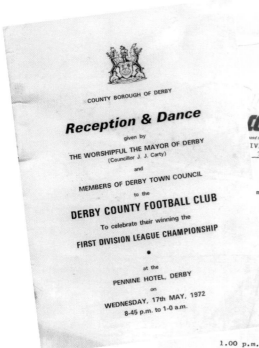

Reception & Dance

given by

THE WORSHIPFUL THE MAYOR OF DERBY
(Councillor J. J. Carty)

and

MEMBERS OF DERBY TOWN COUNCIL

to the

DERBY COUNTY FOOTBALL CLUB

To celebrate their winning the

FIRST DIVISION LEAGUE CHAMPIONSHIP

•

at the

PENNINE HOTEL, DERBY

on

WEDNESDAY, 17th MAY, 1972
8-45 p.m. to 1-0 a.m.

COUNTY FOOTBALL CLUB LIMITED

used to the Secretary   Registered in England No. 49139

IVIC RECEPTION TO CELEBRATE THE WINNING OF
THE FOOTBALL LEAGUE CHAMPIONSHIP 1975

DATE: THURSDAY, 8TH MAY, 1975

m.   Officials and wives and Players' wives
                      depart The Baseball Ground for the
                      Council House by Coach.

                      Team Coach departs The Baseball Ground
                      with Team and Chairman for ceremonial
                      procession through streets of Derby
                      on route to the Council House.

                      Reception at The Council House for
                      Directors, Management and Players.

                      End Of Reception at The Council House.

                      Official Party moves on to The Pennine
                      Hotel, Derby.

                      Buffet Reception and Dance at The Pennine
                      Hotel.

1.00 p.m.   Carriages.

N.B.   Invited guest not travelling on the Official
       Coach from The Baseball Ground

P/FL

An Agreement made the _____ First

day of _____ 19 78 between _____ A.S.Webb
        August   Derbyshire
of _____ The Baseball Ground _____ in the County of _____
the Secretary of and acting pursuant to Resolution and Authority for and on behalf
of the _____ Derby County _____ FOOTBALL CLUB of The Baseball Ground
(hereinafter referred to as the Club) of the one part and
                    Roy Leslie McFarland
of _____ 14 Woodlands Lane , Quarndon, Derby
in the County of _____ Derbyshire _____ Football Player
(hereinafter referred to as the Player) of the other part w h e r e b y it is agreed
as follows :—

1. The Player hereby agrees to play in an efficient manner and to the best of his
ability for the Club for the period of _____ One _____ (year/years) (hereinafter called
"the initial period of employment") from the _____ First _____ day of
August 78 _____ to the 30th day of June 31/7/79 . Unless the initial period of
employment shall either be (a) previously determined in accordance with the provisions of one or other of Clauses 10, 11 or 12 hereof or (b) terminated, extended
or renewed as provided by Clauses 17 and 18 of this Agreement.

2. The Player shall attend the Club's ground or any other place decided upon by
the Club for the purposes of or in connection with his training as a Player pursuant
to the instructions of the Secretary, Manager, or Trainer of the Club, or of such
other person, or persons as the Club may appoint.

3. The Player shall do everything necessary to get and keep himself in the best
possible condition so as to render the most efficient service to the Club, and will
carry out all the training and other instructions of the Club through its representative officials.

4. The Player shall observe and be subject to all the Rules, Regulations and
Bye-Laws of The Football Association, and any other Association, League, or
Combination of which the Club shall be a member. And this Agreement shall be
subject to any action which shall be taken by The Football Association under
their Rules for the suspension or termination of the Football Season, and if any
such suspension or termination shall be decided upon the payment of wages shall
likewise be suspended or terminated, as the case may be and in any proceedings by
the Player against the Club it shall be a sufficient and complete defence and
answer by and on the part of the Club that such suspension or termination hereof
is due to the action of The Football Association, or any Sub-Committee thereof to
whom the power may be delegated.

5. The Player shall not engage in any business or live in any place which the
Directors (or Committee) of the Club may deem unsuitable.

6. Unless this Agreement has previously been determined by any one of Clauses
10, 11 or 12 hereof as hereinafter provided, the Player shall not before the last
day of the playing season next preceding the expiration of any further or additional
further period for which this Agreement shall have been renewed in accordance
with the provisions of Clauses 17 or 18 hereof or before the last day of the playing

with the Football League trophy one Sunday morning in May 1972. The photograph is taken from the corner of the Baseball Hotel looking down Shaftesbury Crescent and you can see the old-fashioned flood-lights and the terraced houses opposite the ground.

The Baseball Ground, Chairman S. LONGSON

As other clubs sent their congratulations to the club on their winning the League, a card was printed that was sent back in acknowledgement.

On 8 May 1975 there was an open-top bus tour round the streets of Derby, arriving at the Council House for a Civic Reception. The trip was to start at 6.45pm from the Baseball Ground, stopping for the reception and then moving on to the Pennine Hotel.

Player's contract

Roy McFarland's last contract before his

departure at the end of the 1980–81 season was negotiated in 1979 and was a two-year contract that had a basic wage of £450 per week in the first year and £500 per week in the second year.

Specific clauses relate to pension payments, him writing a piece for the programme, various loyalty payments during the two years as well as being entitled to the usual bonus payments (points, appearances, cup runs, attendances and League positions).

Dave Mackay

As we have seen already (1969 Division Two Championship medal, 1975 Charity Shield plaque), Dave Mackay put the majority of his medals and trophies up for sale some time ago.

Other items sold were:

The Derby County Player of the Year Award for the 1970–71 season, Mackay's last with Derby.

This is an inscribed electroplated trophy ('The Mecca Cup') and stands 12 inches tall.

The 9ct gold Championship-winners plaque from the 1974–75 season that is inscribed 'Division 1 Champions, D.C. Mackay, Manager, Derby County F.C.'

The Bell's Whisky Manager of the Year Award for the 1974–75 season, which is an electroplated salver, approximately 10 inches in diameter and inscribed with the year, manager's name and club.

Ramtique

With European football, League Championships and famous players, there was a constant demand for all types of official merchandise. This ranged from ceramic pieces produced by local pottery companies to mugs and patches.

The overwhelming demand for players' autographs was met head-on with the production of the pre-printed autograph sheet that was sent out at every request. Other items stocked were the Rammie banks and tankards.

To commemorate the winning of the first Championship, a numbered, limited edition silver goblet was made. This one is number 23 and is in one of the trophy cabinets.

Roger Davies and David Nish met each other as teammates at Derby and became firm friends. They put their name to a football-based board game called Top Club Soccer. As with most board games of this type, there were many small plastic pieces and large amounts of paper money.

Chapter Eight
The 1980s

The 1980s kicked off amid some optimism, with the 'We'll be back in '81' slogan. The reality of the situation showed itself at the first game, Derby's first visit to Cambridge, in a thumping 3–0 defeat. Many of the previous year's staff had been sold, including Daly, Langan and Biley, and Roy McFarland announced that he would be leaving at the end of the season. Kevin Hector returned in an unfamiliar midfield position and without ever challenging the top places, sixth position was secured.

A fundamental change in football occurred during the close season, when three points for a win was introduced. Results did not improve and by the end of the season Addison had been replaced by his assistant John Newman as the manager. Kevin Hector officially retired after the last game against Watford, in which he scored a crucial goal. A 16th place finish was secured, but attendances were at a post-war low of an average 11,800. In an attempt to raise cash the public were offered shares for the first time, at £10 each.

Following a run of five successive defeats, with attendances dipping to 8,000 and Derby bottom of the League, Peter Taylor came out of retirement to take over the club. Roy McFarland returned as his assistant from Bradford City amid poaching claims and investigations. In the FA Cup, Derby had beaten Nottingham Forest in a Taylor v Clough encounter and were eventually knocked out by Manchester United. A 15-match unbeaten run saw the team finish in 13th place and controversy came as the last game against Fulham had to be abandoned due to a crowd invasion with time still to be played.

The season of 1983–84 was very nearly the last, as a deepening financial crisis meant that bills were not paid and the Inland Revenue placed a winding-up order before the High Court. By mid-March a cup run that brought in much needed money had come to an end at the hands of Plymouth Argyle in a replay at the Baseball Ground, with Watford waiting in the semi-final, and relegation was also a probability. On the same evening it was announced that a potential buyer for the club, Robert Maxwell, had reconsidered and withdrawn. Two weeks later agreement with Maxwell had been reached and the case was dismissed from the court. Peter Taylor was sacked and McFarland put in charge until the summer, when relegation was confirmed and Derby would be playing their centenary season in Division Three.

Arthur Cox, a strong character with a philosophy built on hard work, honesty and discipline, left promoted Newcastle to join Derby as manager, keeping McFarland as his assistant. His first task was to find some players, as many had departed during the summer, and with a lack of money, many free transfers were brought in. Kevin Wilson (14 goals in 17 games) was sold to Ipswich Town to finance the purchase of Trevor Christie, Gary Micklewhite and Geraint Williams. A shock exit at Hartlepool in the first round of the FA Cup was put behind the Rams as they finished seventh and gave hope for the future with a better squad of players.

Promotion the following year, in third place, was sealed with a wet Friday night victory over Rotherham United with goals from the emerging Phil Gee and a Christie penalty. The signing of England International John Gregory from QPR in November was the crucial turning point. The reserve team also won the Central League, a remarkable effort for a Third Division team.

The 1986–87 season was expected to have been one of consolidation and, after the opening day defeat at home to Oldham, a mid-table place would have been acceptable. The additions to the squad of Sage, Forsyth and Callaghan and a record-breaking 11 away wins saw the Second Division Championship won outright.

England internationals Peter Shilton and Mark Wright were purchased from Southampton as chairman Robert Maxwell demanded average attendances in excess of 20,000 in return. Ten successive defeats between December and February meant that was unlikely to happen and the true figure was 17,300.

The highest League finish since 1975 placed Derby fifth, with the help of goals from Derby's million-pound player Dean Saunders, from Maxwell-owned Oxford United, and Paul Goddard from Newcastle. Derby were the only team to do the double over champions Arsenal.

Maxwell's interest and money soon dried up and the club were faced with a long injury list throughout the 1989–90 season, which hindered their progress. They survived relegation by just three points.

Books

In 1983 Breedon Books produced the first detailed book covering the history of the club from its foundation and highlighted some of the famous players whose names and achievements had long since been forgotten, finding pictures of teams and players buried in the archives of the local newspapers and photographers. *The Derby County Story* was written by Anton Rippon and Andrew Ward and was an A4-size, 100-page softback released to coincide with the club's centenary in 1984. This was the first in a long line of football books produced by Breedon Books. For the first time, overall player records were collated and this sparked an interest in former players and the history of clubs.

Peter Seddon's *A Football Compendium*, itself an impressive book that lists every football book ever published until 1999, called the *Derby County Complete Record* a 'landmark publication in modern football publishing'. This book, published in 1984, is recognised by many as the start of the boom in football book publishing, as a series of similar books was produced for many clubs and firmly established Breedon Books, a Derby-based company, at the forefront of football-book publishing.

There was also the innovation of asking supporters to pay in advance for a copy of the book that had a special numbered sticker inside and also put the subscriber's name in the back of the book, a format that has been used on a number of occasions since by various publishers. Originally these subscriber copies were available for £11.95.

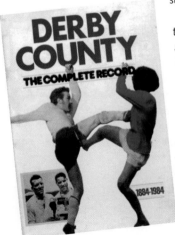

The picture on the front of the dust jacket leaves something to be desired and, with a whole library of photographs available, a better one could surely have been found. The series of books became highly collectable throughout the country as a whole and the early editions are particularly sought after. Many were released to coincide with the club's centenary and many ageing, forgotten, former players have signed copies of the books, adding to their value. Compiled by Gerald Mortimer, with the help of Mike Wilson, John Grainger and Andrew Ward, and edited by Anton Rippon, the *Complete Record* was a remarkable piece of work, cross-referencing details held at the Football League headquarters (then in Lytham St Annes) with contemporary newspaper reports and various club historians around the country.

Given the amount of work in compiling the match-by-match results and researching player biographies, there were inevitably some details that were not immediately available or articles that had to be omitted from the first edition of the *Complete Record*. A supplement was published in 1985. Whether the original intention was to issue an update at the end of every season is not known, but no other updates have followed so soon after the original publication, making it quite a rarity. The years after the first edition of the *Complete Record* had seen other books published in the series and, using the ideas and experience gained from these others, an update of the Derby book was undertaken in 1988, this time including biographies of all players and more 'Great Matches', updated statistics and more photographs.

As a direct result of the *Compete Record* book, various parts of it were expanded into more detailed books in their own right, examples being the *Who's Who* (now in its second incarnation, September 2004), *Great Matches*, *Images of*, *Famous Players* and so on, although one wonders how many times the same details can be rewritten and repackaged without boring the intended audience.

The official centenary book, *There Was Some Football Too* by TV reporter Tony Francis took a media perspective of the club through its turbulent years, with very little coverage on the first 85 years of the club's history. On the field events take a back seat while the author explains the Clough departure, bankruptcy, Mackay and Maxwell, ending in the High Court. It is an interesting book, but a strange choice to be the official centenary publication.

The Brian Clough and Peter Taylor partnership has produced a total of five books over a number of years, starting with the Peter Taylor book *With Clough by Taylor* in 1980, and there have been two biographies (*His Way* by Pat Murphy and *Clough* by Tony Francis) as well as autobiographies *Clough: The Autobiography* in 1994 and *Walking on Water* in 2002. Since his death in September 2004, there has been a renewed interest in these books, particularly the earlier and signed ones.

Tim Ward's story is told in the book *Armed with a Football,* which was written by his son Andrew. It covers his early years as well as life as a professional football player with Derby County and England, before moving into management. It is a fascinating recollection of how football and family life mixed during Andrew's younger years.

The Arthur Cox-led promotion teams of the mid-1980s brought further special, official promotion publications. The first, celebrating the 1986 promotion with the title *We're going up!*, contained pictures and details of all the games and interviews with the squad and directors in its 32 pages. Twelve months later *3-2-1 Back in the Big Time* followed the same format, expanded to 40 pages, with colour pictures of the players.

First-day covers

1987 saw the island of St Vincent produce a number of covers for various First Division clubs, and these also had a special stamp featuring the playing squad. Sheets of the stamps, which just carry the squad picture, were also produced. These are quite common and many dealers will have them.

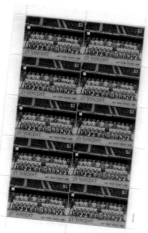

Sunderland produced their own special cover that marked the 100th League meeting between the two clubs in February 1987. These were limited to 500 and most of them have at least one signature on the front. Inside is a sheet with a brief statistical summary of the history of matches between the clubs and players that have played for both.

Commemorative First Day Cover

The Football League's centenary was in 1988, and in association with Dawn Covers it produced a special commemorative cover showing the founder members of the League, with each having a unique stamp and details of the honours won.

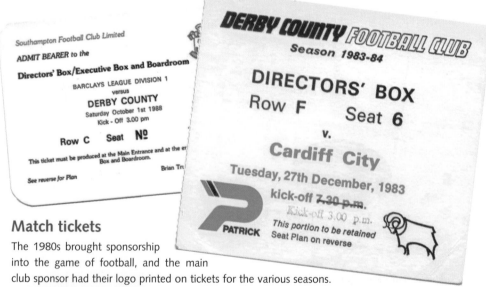

Match tickets

The 1980s brought sponsorship into the game of football, and the main club sponsor had their logo printed on tickets for the various seasons.

The introduction of computerised ticketing printers meant that a standard layout could be decided upon during the close season and this allowed the majority of the tickets to be pre-printed with just the fixture details added for each game.

Special directors tickets were also used, which had a seating plan of the Directors' Box on the reverse and were card instead of paper.

The mid-1980s saw many of Derby's away matches declared all-ticket events. This was because as Derby suffered relegation into the Third Division, the number of people who wished to follow them to some of the less glamourous stadia around the country, some for the first time, seemed to increase. This often reached a point when the numbers wanting to travel was greater than the capacity of the away ground and authorities to cope with.

Luton Town also attempted to introduce a ban on all away supporters, by making entry to their matches 'members only'. They were also among those clubs that had a plastic pitch installed and used credit card-sized plastic cards to allow you entry into the ground by the computerised turnstiles.

Fanzines

The latter part of the 1980s saw supporters of many clubs produce their own magazine to put alternative views to those put out by the club in the official matchday programmes and other publications, and gave supporters the ability to criticise their club and its on and off-field activities. These fanzines were hugely popular at some clubs and are still produced today. National magazines such as *When Saturday Comes*, started in 1986, encouraged the production of the independent supporters' magazines around the country. They were filled with a mixture of humour, criticism and information and also tried to deal with issues that were affecting supporters such as all-seater stadia, away fan exclusion from matches and identity cards.

One of Derby's first fanzine publications, *The Derby County Programme Collectors Review*, was produced in February/March 1987 by Moz Curtin, aimed mainly at the collectors of matchday programmes and those interested in the history of the club, and it was renamed as *Bloomer Shoots…Shilton Saves* in August 1989 to reflect the magazine's historical bias as well as more modern issues.

Another of the early fanzines was *The Sheep* in late 1989, which throughout its time was filled with adverts. The first issue contained many articles taken from Breedon's *Complete Record* book, while readers' letters and contributions were awaited.

Tapes

As the club reached its centenary and progressed through from the Third to the First Division, the local radio station, BBC Radio Derby, produced a number of audio cassette tapes that featured the story of the season and had commentary clips of many of the important goals and events.

The *Derby County Story* was a weekly series originally broadcast from

September to December 1984, and the 15 parts were condensed down onto two cassettes and issued in a numbered, limited edition boxed set.

Other cassette tapes were produced for the promotion seasons of 1985–86 and 1986–87.

Videos

Video tapes were starting to appear of individual matches as well as season highlights packages. During the 1980s there was the Betamax and VHS battle, and video tapes were produced in both formats, before the Betamax standard disappeared.

The promotion match from Division Three against Rotherham United on a wet Friday night is one of those that was produced in both formats, but it is unlikely that many copies survive.

Ramtastic was one of the first videos that looked back at some of the famous television

matches involving Derby from the 1971–1976 period. The sleeve will look familiar to FKS sticker collectors, as it is the same picture that was used on the front of one of the FKS sticker albums in the 1970s. The back of the sleeve has various FKS pictures.

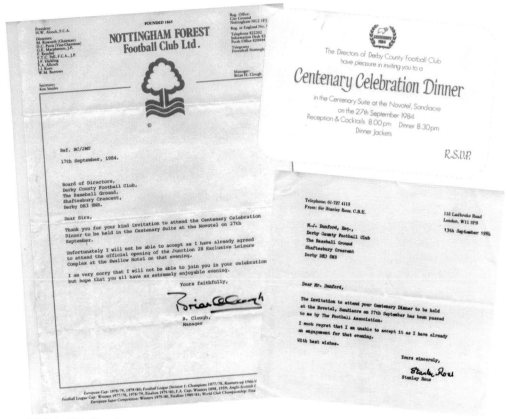

1984–85 Centenary season

The turmoil of the previous season, which saw the club in the High Court facing a winding-up order, the disappointment of losing at home to Plymouth Argyle in the sixth round of the FA Cup, the loss of manager Peter Taylor and relegation to the third tier of English League football, meant that the centenary season started off in a bad way. Arthur Cox surprisingly left promoted Newcastle United to take charge and had to recruit many players on free transfers to be able to field a team at the start of the season.

Throughout the year there were many special events, culminating in a Centenary Dinner that took place on 27 September 1984 at the Novotel at Sandiacre.

Many famous names from the world of football were invited, along with many ex-players and managers. Two who were unable to attend due to prior engagements were Brian Clough and Sir Stanley Rous, who sent their written apologies.

The Queen is well known for sending a telegram to individuals celebrating their 100th birthday and she did the same for the football club. This was sent to the dinner and reads 'Her Majesty the Queen extends all good wishes to the members of Derby County Football Club on the occasion of the club's centenary and acknowledges their loyal greetings'. This was found in one of the many

COMMERCIAL AGREEMENT

It is hereby agreed that BASS WORTHINGTON LIMITED will enter into a corporate sponsorship package including shirt advertising with DERBY COUNTY FOOTBALL CLUB p.l.c. for two years commencing August 1984.

SIGNED FOR AND ON BEHALF OF
DERBY COUNTY FOOTBALL CLUB p.l.c. ....

SIGNED FOR AND ON BEHALF OF
BASS WORTHINGTON LTD. ....

DATE ....

The Baseball Ground, Derby DE3 8NB   Telephone: Derby 40105/6/7   Grams: FOOTBALL DERBY

boxes of papers in a storeroom behind the gents' toilets underneath the 'C' Stand area at the Baseball Ground and is now at Pride Park.

Real Madrid, one of Derby's opponents in the European Cup in the 1970s, sent Derby a specially engraved silver tray with the Bernabeau Stadium and Real Madrid logos on the tray with an engraved inscription.

Local brewer Bass became the club's main sponsor for the following two years, during which their logo appeared on the shirts and on tickets and match programmes.

Special one-season shirts were produced for the centenary that incorporated the original club colours of brown, blue and amber in a stripe on the shoulder. The shirts were made by Admiral and cost £13.99 for a large mens size. The away shirt was a blue colour and sold for the same price.

There were many other collectables that carried the centenary logo, from scarves, beer glasses and mugs to silver spoons.

For this special season the programme cover incorporated the club's first colours of amber, blue and chocolate. There was also a new club logo, with the wording 'Centenary 1984' underneath the ram. The 24 pages cost 50p and the three old colours appeared regularly throughout the publication, including the centre pages featuring a player profile with a full-page picture. This particular edition, versus Rotherham United, shows the special Centenary Commemorative scroll of honour presented by the Football

Association and details the club's record of the 100 years and lists all the players capped by the Home Countries and Ireland while registered with Derby.

Bass Worthington were the club's main sponsor throughout the centenary season and as part of the partnership they produced a limited edition ale in half-pint bottles with special labels. According to the press release, the limited edition nature of the ale means that it was only produced once and was available from 27 April 1984 in local Bass pubs until it all sold out.

As the press release says, fans were faced with a dilemma – what do you do with your bottle of ale; drink it or keep it unopened? Probably the best answer was to buy two bottles!

Programmes

The decade started with the usual *Ram* newspaper as the main matchday publication, but as a struggle to avoid relegation continued, attendances naturally declined and so did the circulation.

The newspaper for the 1980–81 season had 16 pages and its price had increased to 30p. It was slightly narrower than the previous nine volumes and the other noticeable change was that the team line-ups included a 2-3 line description of each player and his current form.

Programmes from the early part of the 1982–83 season are quite hard to find, as Derby struggled at the bottom of the League. Attendances were not very high, the print run was reduced and there is now a demand for some of these issues, especially Middlesbrough, Leicester City and Chelsea. This was to be the last season the newspaper format was used.

The traditional programme was produced, consisting of 24 pages and costing 50p. In that 24 pages, there was an eight-page insert, called *Centrespot*, used by a number of clubs to bulk out programmes, which offered lots of reading with very few adverts.

The 1986–87 programme was called *Ram Magazine* and has a full colour picture on the front cover as well as fixture details and has main sponsor and match sponsor logos. For this season a new feature called 'Rams Showcase' generally featured an item from the trophy cabinets with the story that goes with it. Some excellent photographs of past historical items made this an enjoyable article. Good historical content by the ever-present Mike Wilson and many pictures made this a leading programme for the Division.

Many of the friendly matches played at home did not have a full programme printed for them and normally a teamsheet was given away upon entry. Even the introduction of an annual match against Chesterfield for the Derbyshire Centenary Cup did not warrant a programme. Probably the rarest of these teamsheets is for the pre-season match against Sunderland in August 1982. An unusual sized teamsheet (10x8in) on a green background was issued and is undated.

Club kit

By the 1980s the suppliers of the team and replica kit were used to having two-year contracts that basically kept the kits the same for that period. As usual, each change brought new ideas, trim and colours for the shirts, and some strange designs for the away kits.

As with most shirts, the official players' shirts will have an embroidered club badge and the replica will just be printed onto the shirt.

The shirt manufacturers realised there was a potential market in the sale of replicas, and the 1980 manufacturer Le Coq Sportif produced replica shirts that cost from £7.99 at the Ramtique. These were the first sponsored shirts, with the slogan 'Fly British Midland' on the front.

Patrick were the next suppliers and they reversed the way the ram was facing and positioned it centrally. For the first four years of the 1980s the away kit was an orange-coloured shirt.

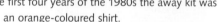
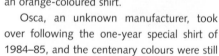

Osca, an unknown manufacturer, took over following the one-year special shirt of 1984–85, and the centenary colours were still incorporated around the collar and sleeves. The away shirt was now a two-tone blue striped shirt with white trim.

Umbro, probably the largest kit supplier, took over the contract and produced a predominately plain white shirt with Maxwell as the main sponsor on the front.

For the 1988–89 season the change kit became a blue checkerboard shirt that was only used for one year.

The Annual General Meeting held in November 1988 saw the unveiling of the new kit and the change from blue back to the traditional black shorts. This had the universal approval of the shareholders. The away kit, however, resembled a barcode with grey and black stripes. The cost of the replica shirt had now risen to over £20.

Match notes

One unique feature of the Arthur Cox years as manager was the amount of detail that he, and his management team, kept in relation to each match played by the first, reserve and

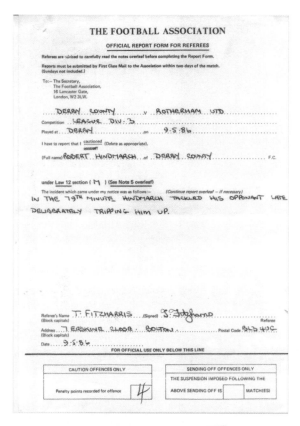

youth teams. For each match, both Cox and assistant Roy McFarland completed a form that marked players for their performance and also had space for any comments. The last match of the season was against Plymouth Argyle, and their comments indicate that the first half was the worst performance of the season and in the second half the team 'looked strong and very competitive'. Both Cox and McFarland comment that the central-defensive pair of Hindmarch and MacLaren were nervous or over-confident and let the occasion get to them. This comment applied to a number of people, and Callaghan was selected by the management as the best player. Many of these match notes were sold during the official auctions of 2003 as various Baseball Ground offices were cleared.

Every time a player is booked during a game, the referee has to submit a written report to the Football Association detailing the circumstances of the offence. The match against Rotherham United on 9 May 1986 saw Derby promoted to the Second Division courtesy of a late Trevor Christie penalty. During the game Rob Hindmarch was booked and the form was completed by the referee, Mr Fitzharris.

Season tickets

The 1980s saw a number of different season-ticket books used, as new technology was being tried to speed up entry into the stadium. The usual ticket was used for a number of years and a new credit card-style season ticket was tried (see the examples from 1987–88), but it was not a success and the following year a larger (twice the size), computer-printed ticket book was issued.

The season ticket renewal documents give an indication of how prices increase year on

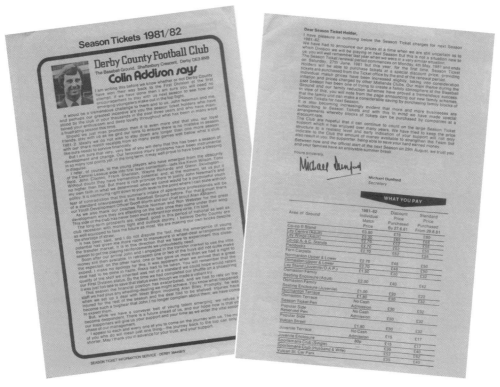

year and also the views of the manager in attempting to persuade the supporter to part with his money. For 1981–82 Colin Addison wrote a full A4 page explaining the season's performance and issues relating to players for the coming season. The best price seats, in 'B' Stand, were £80, with a terrace ticket, £32. By the end of the decade, with a team containing Saunders, Shilton and Wright, the same tickets cost £175 and £85 respectively.

Fixture cards

As corporate sponsorship came into football, various pages in programmes, shirts, tickets and fixture cards began carrying logos and adverts. The fixture card was redesigned and was made a single card, folded into three (13½x8cm), of which the additional two sides carried advertising. Seat prices were also included, which ranged from £2 to £3.80. By the mid-1980s the card had gone back to a double-sided card, with the print condensed on the fixture lists, so the back cover could carry the main sponsor's message. By the end of the decade the card had been reduced to a single card (10x8cm) and fitted in with the change in size of the season-ticket book.

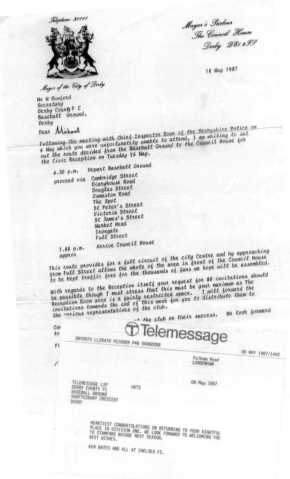

1986–87 Champions

The 1986–87 season saw the club win the title and with it the *Today* League trophy, which has been retained by the club as the only winners. The City Council wished to commemorate the achievement by holding a civic reception at the Council House, preceded by a bus tour from the Baseball Ground to the Council House of the players and management. In the archives are the letter from the Mayor's Parlour regarding the bus route to be taken and agreed with the local police, and the telegram from Mr Ken Bates at Chelsea sending his congratulations on promotion and looking forward to meeting the Rams next season.

Model van

A number of die-cast models have been produced with the Derby County name and logo painted on the side. This Model T Ford was produced in 1983 as a promotional model by Lledo and issued by Eastwood Promotional Marketing. Each was a limited edition of 2,200, and issued with a certificate.

Accounts

Following a public share issue in 1982, many supporters became shareholders of the club, initially paying £10 per share. As with any investment in football clubs, one should not expect to get anything back from it financially, but annual reports and accounts and invites to the Annual General Meeting were the only benefit.

The report and annual accounts for 1987 shows the Division Two trophy on the cover and inside

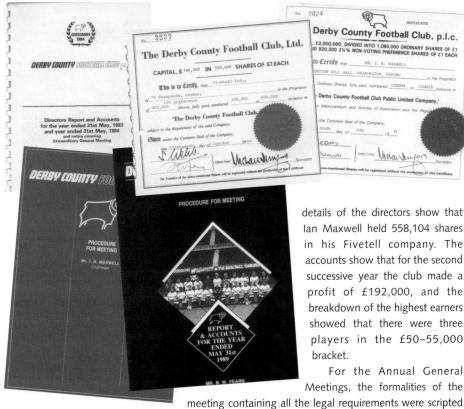

details of the directors show that Ian Maxwell held 558,104 shares in his Fivetell company. The accounts show that for the second successive year the club made a profit of £192,000, and the breakdown of the highest earners showed that there were three players in the £50–55,000 bracket.

For the Annual General Meetings, the formalities of the meeting containing all the legal requirements were scripted in advance and printed in books for the chairman to read. This, from 1988, was I.R. Maxwell's copy (Robert Maxwell's actual name was Ian Robert Maxwell, not be confused with his son Ian Robert Charles Maxwell, who was also a chairman of the club).

Transfer list

Before the days of football agents, email and internet and player databases, when a player was put on the transfer list the club spent some time preparing a file so that it could be circulated by post or

fax to any potential interested parties. This detail included the player's career information and the contact details should anyone be interested. Examples show one from 1980 for Keith Osgood that has a photograph of the player and also the 1985 Eric Steele version.

Cards and stickers

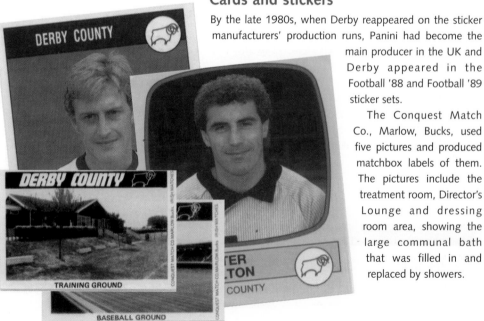

By the late 1980s, when Derby reappeared on the sticker manufacturers' production runs, Panini had become the main producer in the UK and Derby appeared in the Football '88 and Football '89 sticker sets.

The Conquest Match Co., Marlow, Bucks, used five pictures and produced matchbox labels of them. The pictures include the treatment room, Director's Lounge and dressing room area, showing the large communal bath that was filled in and replaced by showers.

Chapter Nine
The 1990s

The World Cup Finals in Italy during the summer of 1990 saw Peter Shilton and Mark Wright play major parts in getting England through to the semi-finals, before the penalty shoot-out disappointment. Within the first few months of the 1990–91 season. Robert Maxwell had put the club back up for sale, with no obvious candidates coming in to take control. There were some strange results that season: a 6–0 victory over Sunderland in the Rumbelows (League) Cup, a 4–6 defeat at home to Chelsea in a game that saw Derby come back from a 1–3 scoreline to be winning 4–3 with a little over 10 minutes to play, and an astonishing 1–7 home defeat to Liverpool. Frustration around the club was growing, not with the management or players, but with Mr Maxwell, who appeared to have lost all interest in the club.

Relegation was inevitable, as was the sale of Wright and Dean Saunders to Liverpool, but a slide in the valuation of the club meant a sale in June 1991 could be concluded. By November, Lionel Pickering had become the majority shareholder and cleared the debts and made a huge investment in young English players that Arthur Cox hoped would gel into a formidable team. Gabbiadini, Simpson, Sutton, Kitson and Johnson were signed and created a club record of 12 away wins during a season, but were let down by an average home record. A play-off place was secured, although with 13 minutes of the regular season to play, the scores around the country had given Derby a brief automatic promotion place. The two-leg play-off was against Blackburn Rovers, but defensive errors in the first leg meant the deficit could not be overturned and eventually Derby lost 4–5 on aggregate.

More signings were to follow, including Pembridge, Short and Wassall, but the results followed a similar pattern: winning away games but losing at home.

There was a Cup Final appearance in the 1992–93 season in the Anglo-Italian Cup, but no silverware was won as Italian team Cremonese won comfortably 1–3 at Wembley. Overall 64 games had been played during the season and playing resources were stretched.

Arthur Cox, who had been manager for over nine years, had a severe back injury that saw him relinquish control temporarily to Roy McFarland, before having to resign in October 1993. After a topsy-turvy set of results, a play-off place was secured and Millwall awaited Derby in the semi-finals. A comfortable 2–0 win in the home leg and a 3–1 win in London led to another Wembley appearance against local rivals Leicester City. The return leg at Millwall will not be remembered for the scoreline, but for the pitch invasions and attacks on Derby players by the notorious Millwall fans. The Final was lost three minutes from time and a play-off-experienced Leicester side gained promotion.

Lionel Pickering used his majority shareholding to take over as chairman early in the 1994–95 season. The cost of not gaining promotion began to bite as many of the players (Kitson, Johnson and Charles) were sold at a profit and more new players were brought in, 33 different ones being used during the season. A poor run-in saw a potential play-off place reduced to a ninth-place finish, and as a result manager McFarland's contract was not renewed at the end of the season.

During the summer of 1995, the Popular Side terracing had been removed and replaced by ranks of new seating to fall in line with the Taylor Report, making it an all-seater stadium for the first time.

The decision had also been made to redevelop the Baseball Ground site instead of relocating to elsewhere in the city. Jim Smith was appointed the new manager, an old-school type of manager that had been around for many years. Three major players left immediately – Pembridge, Short and Williams – and Smith brought in some workman-like performers from various Divisions. By November, Derby were an average team lying in 15th place, and Igor Stimac was bought from Hadjuk Split. Suddenly everything fell into place, as the team won 10 out of the next 11 matches and Derby went to the top of the table. An announcement in February 1996 reversed the previous summer's decision to rebuild the Baseball Ground and a new stadium would be completed for the start of the 1997–98 season at Pride Park. A 2–1 victory over Crystal Palace in the penultimate match of the season saw promotion to the Premier League guaranteed.

The first season in the Premier League was always going to be difficult and this was also the last season of League football at the Baseball Ground. The FA Cup provided a highlight of the season that saw a run to the quarter-finals and a game against Middlesbrough, with Chesterfield waiting in the semi-final. Probably the most memorable game was at Old Trafford, where Derby fielded new signings Poom (the Estonian goalkeeper) and Wanchope (from Costa Rica) in an astonishing 3–2 win. The final game at the Baseball Ground was on 11 May 1997 against Arsenal where a host of former players came along.

Pride Park Stadium was officially opened by the Queen in July 1997, before the first game against Sampdoria of Italy on 4 August. The first League game at the new stadium had to be abandoned as a floodlight failure brought an end after 56 minutes. Stefano Eranio, a summer import from Italy, became the first scorer of a Derby goal at the new stadium, a penalty against Barnsley.

1998–99 saw Derby reach their highest Premier League finish of eighth and almost all the victories were by a one-goal margin. A good cup run came to an end at Arsenal, where the Rams lost to a very late goal in the sixth round. The top scorers during the season were Burton and Wanchope, both with nine goals. There were signs that things were starting to go wrong, as first-team coach Steve McClaren left to join Manchester United and the player signings of Borbokis and Beck summed up the direction of the club.

The millennium season saw a slide to 16th place and the pre-season saw Stimac and Wanchope leave for West Ham United. A lengthy transfer of Argentinian Esteban Fuertes had a long-term effect, culminating in the player not being allowed entry into the UK following a break due to passport irregularities. Significant transfers that took place were the purchase of Craig Burley from Celtic, an unfit Kinkladze from Ajax, Morris from Sheffield United and Strupar from Belgium. Young reserve players started to make a breakthrough – Riggott, Jackson, Boertien, Elliott and Christie. Branko Strupar had the honour of scoring the fastest goal of the new millennium in a 2–0 win against Watford.

Books

A rewrite of the *Derby County Story* was completed in 1991, with the addition of Gerald Mortimer to the list of authors. The book was hugely expanded to include the Maxwell years and included many historical details not previously included. Technological advancements in the publishing industry allowed better photographic reproduction and layout in the 256 pages, which also had a subscriber section. A further revision and update followed in 1998, which included the promotion to the Premier League and the move from the Baseball Ground to the Pride Park Stadium. The text and pictures remained largely unchanged, although some of the pictures were resized.

Edward Giles is yet another former *Derby Evening Telegraph* sports reporter turned author. Using his extensive knowledge, personal records and access to the picture archives at the paper, he has written four books to date relating to previously less well documented periods in the Rams' history. Starting with *Derby County Days* he covers the period from 1944 to 1956, which includes the FA Cup win and decline into the Third Division. *Journeys with Jobey* covers the 1925 season to the closedown of professional football due to the war and *Bloomer and Before* covers the formation of the club as part of the cricket club to the Jobey years of the 1920s. His latest book, published in 2005, is called *Champions and England*.

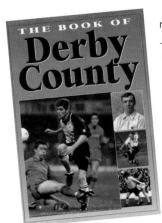

Ian Hall, a player from 1959 to 1962, and more recently a local radio summariser, has written three books to date. His first was *Journey Through a Season*, in which he follows Derby around the country in their first Premiership season during 1996–97.

Two other Breedon editions that expanded on sections in the Complete Record are *The Book of Derby County* (1994) and *The Great Days of Derby County* (1993), edited by Anton Rippon. The former book looks at specific subject areas in detail, such as encounters against local rivals Nottingham Forest, matches on Christmas Day, in-depth profiles of players including Raich Carter and sponsored competitions. These subjects are given much more coverage than allowed in previous books and the *Great Days* looks at famous matches in the history of the club, from an 1885 victory against Aston Villa through to a 3–3 FA Cup match against Sheffield Wednesday in 1993, with the majority of the book concentrating on the period from 1967 when Brian Clough took over as manager and the club entered into its longest sustained period of success.

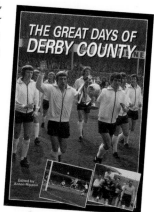

The area of land that was the Baseball Ground was first used to stage football matches in 1892 and became the permanent home to the club from 1895 to 1997, although reserve and youth-team football continued until 2003. To mark the end of their time there the club produced the book *The Baseball Ground 1895–1997*, which contained a brief stadium history, many memories by supporters and players, the usual list of famous players through the decades, a chapter on the final game against Arsenal in May 1997 and a statistical history relating to matches played there.

In 1999 *Pride Park: The Story of a Stadium* told how the move to Pride Park came about after work on the redevelopment of the Baseball Ground was about to start. Details of the construction with pictures are included and a review of the first two seasons at the new stadium is given. Written by Jim Fearn and Damon Parkin of the club's Press department, it also has the subscriber names included and has a number of adverts in the book, which offset the cost of production.

Smaller publications

There have been numerous other books, some no more than a few pages, which cover a number of subject areas. Having small print runs, these will now be difficult to obtain for the collector.

One of these is *The Derby County Story Told in Pictures* by David Thornton, which is aimed at the juvenile market and contains 16 pages of drawn pictures that cover the early years through to the Cox years of the late 1980s. There are some inaccuracies in the text (e.g. Bloomer being sold to Sunderland instead of Middlesbrough, and the Baseball Ground staged a Cup Final replay and international matches), but it is an interesting addition to the library. *The 25 Year Record*, published by Soccer Book Publishing, was a set of books produced for a number of clubs that repeats the pages from the *Complete Record* or *Rothmans Yearbook* for the period from 1970 to 1995, listing all the results, line-ups, attendance, scorers and League tables for those years. No real information or details appear that have not been published previously.

The Programme Collectors Guide to Derby County Programmes 1949–1996 was produced in 1996. This 64-page book lists all first-team fixtures since 1946 in all competitions, making it a useful resource for all collectors to use as a checklist. It also lists all friendly fixtures, postponements, includes number of programme cover illustrations and a rough price guide. A subsequent booklet was issued that listed the reserve-team fixtures for the same period as well as updating the previous work with new information.

The Mirror Pocket Guide for the 1997–98 season was available only in newsagents, and was only on sale for a short space of time. They can be difficult to find for sale and it is even harder to complete a set, as one was produced for each Premier League club. As the club was just moving into Pride Park, there was confusion in the directory section, with the Baseball Ground phone numbers still being printed.

As the top Division in England gained more international coverage, particularly in Scandanavia and the Far East, publications have also appeared in various countries. As well as a regular Norwegian fanzine, *NorRam*, one of its leading members, Inge Haagensen, also co-wrote the *Derby County 1999–2000* paperback, again one of a set of books covering all the Premier League teams. All in Norwegian, the first 64 pages contain a history, squad details for the millennium season and various 'Top 10' lists. The remainder of the book is the same for all the books in the series, which looks at the English League and has various quotes from players and managers, again translated into Norwegian.

An 18-page booklet was published in Thailand for the 2000–01 season, one of a set in the Soccer Guide Special series for each Premier League club. Not a word of it is in English, but it has pictures of Pride Park, Colin Todd and Brian Clough, as well as some pictures of the squad for that season. Very few of these will have found their way into the UK, and they will not be stocked by any bookshop or programme dealers.

There have also been two quiz books: *The Derby County Centenary Quiz Book*, compiled by Trevor Island in 1985, which was a softback book with over 200 questions contained in its 40 pages, and *The Official Derby County FC Quiz Book*, by Patrick J. Whyte, which was published in 1990 and had many more questions. Each section was headed by a quotation from a Derby player or manager.

The Superclubs Unofficial Yearbook 98–99 was available in local supermarkets and based on a diary-style for the coming season. As similar books were produced for every League team, the majority of the book was the same with only the front few pages being club specific.

A Leicester-based company produced official handbooks for the 1989–90 and 1990–91 seasons. These were A5-sized books of over 140 pages, and the company produced similar books for other Midlands clubs. Selling for £3, these two examples are probably the most complete yearbooks the club has been involved with, containing full squad details, complete statistics for the previous season to youth-team level and a large records section at the back.

We're there! was the souvenir brochure produced for the 1995–96 promotion season, A 68-page full-colour brochure, it has full-page pictures of the players, match-action pictures, statistics and the modern day advertising we have come to expect.

The opening of Pride Park Stadium on 18 July 1997 by the Queen was an opportunity to print a glossy brochure for the event. Although only 20 pages long, it does have details of the new stadium, pictures taken during the construction and player biographies of the squad. Given away free on the day of the opening, there were thousands of copies of these destroyed when the Baseball Ground was sold.

Cards and stickers

The football trade cards had largely died out in the 1980s, being overtaken by the stickers, but new sets produced by Pro-Set in 1990 and 1991 set new standards in photography and reproduction and, although not valuable and easily available, these started a new era of trade card production. The Pro-Set cards feature a number of the major players at the club, including Shilton, Wright and Saunders, and no other trade cards were produced featuring Derby players until their return to the top Division in 1996.

Subbuteo now ventured into cards, producing a game in which player cards were purchased in packets with a seperate box containing the game. There are a number of cards featuring players, one for the manager, Jim Smith, and one of the Baseball

Ground. Others are the unusual Pro-Match cards, in four different series, that are coloured drawings of the players and manager and make for an unusual addition to a collection.

Merlin, who had an exclusive deal to produce cards and stickers for the Premier League, also issued their Premier Gold cards, which are 120-card sets featuring just a few players from each team. Modern production methods also allowed additional 'chase' cards to be produced, which had different foil-type finishes to them. These are harder to obtain than the standard card, and so carry more value.

Pro-Match medals

As well as the cards that Pro-Match produced from 1997 onwards, they also issued a set of 136 'Premiership Medallions'. These feature caricatures of many top Premiership players in a circular picture stuck to a metal disc (having a diameter of 31mm) and were sold in packs of two for 99p. A large, laminated cardboard folder (costing £7.50) enabled these medals to be stuck down and the Derby players featured in the set are Gabbiadini, Stimac and Asanovic.

Stickers

The stickers that were available in the early 1990s were those issued by *The Sun* in 1990–91, Merlin's Team '90 collection and Panini's Football '90 and Football '91 collections.

Panini failed to secure a contract with the Premier League in England, so tried to compete in the English market place by issuing stickers for the Football League in 1995 and 1996, but as they have not been seen since one assumes that these were not a commercial success. A full set of stickers was produced for the Derby squads from those years, and a return to the top Division meant inclusion in the Merlin sticker collections from 1997 onwards. The albums the stickers are designed to be stuck in are huge productions and are extremely good when complete. Various innovations in different sets have seen foil and shiny stickers used.

DEAN SAUNDERS
DERBY COUNTY

DERBY COUNTY

GERAINT WILLIAMS

TREVOR HEBBERD

ROBBIE VAN DER

PAUL SIMPSON

IGOR STIMAC

Merlin Flick-a-Balls

Merlin produced a set of marbles called Flick-a-Ball, which were not a great success. The marbles showed 12 players for each team, each one containing the picture of a player. Their lack of success may make these more rare than the contemporary cards and stickers.

Match tickets

The format of the home match ticket remained unchanged throughout the 1990s until the move to Pride Park Stadium, where a new computerised system was installed that allowed the club to print tickets on demand on a continuous stream of pre-printed stationery.

Many thousands of unused, mint-condition tickets were taken by dealers following the closure of the Baseball Ground, where they were kept for auditing purposes. Any ticket from 1998 onwards will be virtually worthless due to the vast numbers in circulation.

There are a number of unused tickets available from matches played during the last season at the Baseball Ground, which are only available from a couple of sources.

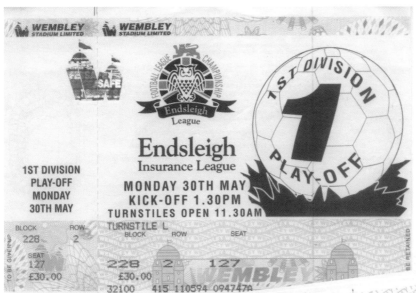

WEMBLEY STADIUM LIMITED   WEMBLEY STADIUM LIMITED

Endsleigh
Insurance League

1ST DIVISION PLAY-OFF

MONDAY 30TH MAY
KICK-OFF 1.30PM
TURNSTILES OPEN 11.30AM

1ST DIVISION
PLAY-OFF
MONDAY
30TH MAY

TURNSTILE L

BLOCK	ROW	BLOCK	ROW	SEAT
228	2			

SEAT
127

228	2	127
£30.00		
£30.00		
£30.00		

32100   415 110594 094747A

DERBY COUNTY FOOTBALL CLUB

DERBY COUNTY
v
EVERTON
SATURDAY 14th DECEMBER 1996
KICK-OFF 3:00 p.m.
FA CARLING PREMIER LEAGUE

ADMIT TO DIRECTORS BOX
JACKET & TIE MUST BE WORN BY MALE GUESTS

ROW: A

ADMIT TO
DIRECTORS
BOX
v
EVERTON
SAT.
14/12/96
3:00pm

THE TOYOTA STAND
CENTRE   CENTRE

THE TOYOTA STAND
CENTRE

CRYSTAL PALACE

SUNDAY 28th APR. 1996
KICK-OFF 3:00 p.m.
ENDSLEIGH INSURANCE
LEAGUE DIVISION ONE
RESTRICTED VIEW

ENTER VIA
TURNSTILE
15-20   15-20

ROW
Q   Q

SEAT
167X   167X

CRYSTAL
PALACE
28/04/96
3:00pm

CRYSTAL
PALACE
28/04/96
3:00pm

RESERVED SEAT
(including VAT)

ADULT
£ 11.00

ADULT
£ 11.00

CONCESSIONARY
£ 6.00

CONCESSIONARY
£ 6.00

£ 11.00
£ 6.00

Keith Loring
Chief Executive
TEL: (01332) 340105

ENTER VIA
TURNSTILE
15-20

GANGWAY
D

THE
TOYOTA
STAND

ROW
Q

SEAT
167X

THIS PORTION TO
BE RETAINED

TO BE GIVEN UP   TO BE GIVEN UP   DERBY COUNTY F.C. LTD. BASEBALL GROUND, DERBY

SECURE   SECURE   SECURE   SECURE

PARK STADIUM
OPENING GAME
DERBY COUNTY
v
SAMPDORIA
14th August 1997
Kick-Off 8:00pm
£7.00 Juv.
FIELD BITTER
STAND UPPER

STAIRWAY
62
SEAT No.   730

55 TO 58
ROW P

These tickets include the last match against Arsenal and unusual ones against Gillingham for an FA Cup replay that did not take place.

Examples shown are: Play-off Final v Leicester City in 1994; Directors' box ticket v Everton in 1996; Directors' box v Chelsea in 1998; Crystal Palace 1996 promotion match; Leeds United in 1996, first match in the Premier League; Gillingham FA Cup replay on 22 January – never played and Directors' ticket v Watford – first game of the new millennium.

Anglo-Italian Cup 1992–93

The Anglo-Italian Cup was originally competed for in the early 1970s, with League teams taking part, but as interest waned it became a non-League competition (Matlock Town competed in the 1979 competition). After a couple of inter-league games between Division Two and Serie B, the competition was resurrected and was by invitation only, and Derby played in three successive years the competition survived.

Of the programmes issued for the games played in England, the qualifying match at Barnsley is probably the hardest

to obtain, being a reduced-size, eight-page black and white issue. Italian clubs are not known for their production of match programmes and the only official items are the photocopied teamsheets available to VIPs and press.

For the first time since the European matches of the 1970s, the club was faced with organising official transport for supporters to some towns in Italy not widely known around Europe.

For the travelling supporter to these away matches, as with any European trip, there are different types of collectable items that could have been purchased or picked up.

These range from the match tickets (see below for Cosenza and Reggiana examples), the Official Itinerary booklet given to those travelling on the official flights, posters and Italian newspapers before and after the matches. The number of travelling supporters to these matches was no more than a couple of hundred, so the availability of any items is going to be limited.

The Final was staged at Wembley and with 60,000 tickets available for Derby fans, of which nearly 37,000 were sold, there is no shortage of ticket stubs for this game. Other interesting items for the Final game are the various advertising leaflets for the special trains, souvenirs from the Ramtique and for the ticket arrangements for the game.

For many people the programme for the Final at Wembley will be the most obvious item to collect, but there were also other items available. Wembley Stadium produced a model of the stadium, mounted on a wooden stand and with a brass-type plaque with the details of the fixture.

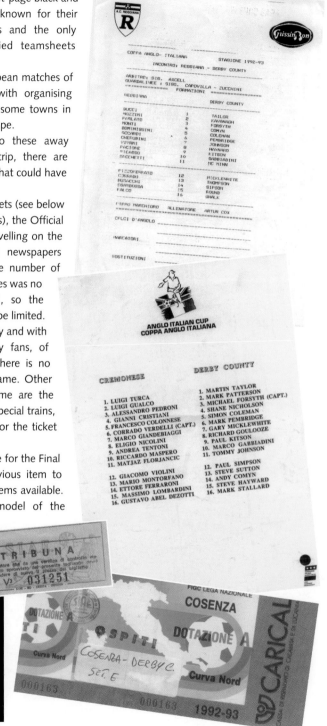

According to the programme this cost £26.50. For those staying in London overnight, there was the opportunity to purchase the Italian football paper *La Gazzetta Sportiva* the following day, which carried a match report and pictures from the Final, with an Italian view of the game.

There was also a special brochure, a 44-page, full-colour edition that featured player profiles, competition details and a historical look back at the previous Wembley appearances.

Although Derby played in the competition for a further two seasons, one encompassing away trips to Ancona and Piacenza, the competition, despite a Wembley Final, was sliding into oblivion.

Corinthian models

The Corinthian player models began to be produced in 1995, initially covering the major players and teams in English football. Derby's promotion to the Premier League meant that contracts were negotiated to produce six Corinthian 'ProStars' models in a Derby playing kit. Each master model was sculptured and painted but they were never commercially produced and sold. This was due to a change in the marketing strategy of Corinthian, who wished to concentrate on major teams whose sales were thought to be stronger across the country. Starting in 2000, these master models were auctioned by the Corinthian Company and are now in the hands of private collectors. The Derby players created were Igor Stimac, Robin Van Der Laan, Sean Flynn, Marco Gabbiadini, Chris Powell and Paul Simpson.

There are some Corinthian collectors and dealers who repaint original models and keep them up-to-date as players are transferred between clubs. Warren Barton and Fabrizio Ravanelli are players that have been repainted in Derby's colours following their transfers. These are totally unofficial models and their value after being repainted is diminished.

Fanzines

The initial success of fanzines across the country continued in Derby, where a number were produced, some better quality than others. These fanzines were written and produced by the fans and depended heavily on the drive and commitment of the editor, who had to find the articles, have contacts for pictures, put together the magazine and get it printed and distributed on a regular basis. Continued production relied heavily on supporters sending in or writing articles for publication. Inevitably, the number of fanzines could not be maintained and many disappeared after only a few issues.

The printing quality varied dramatically between the different fanzines with *The Mutton Mutineer* being a photocopied issue

while others were properly typeset and had correctly reproduced photographs. Some of those produced during the 1990s are *Good Bye Marco*, *Interesting Very Interesting* and *Hey Big Spender*.

August 1991 saw the first issue of *We'll be back in '81!* produced by the Derby County Independent Supporters' Association, a member of the Football Supporters' Association.

C-Stander was probably the best fanzine available, with a wide range of articles, pictures and comment. Some articles were reprinted from the *Derby County Programme Collectors' Review*, which had ceased production.

The longest-running fanzine, *Hey Big Spender*, started in 1992 and continued throughout the decade. Production quality improved over the years.

It is not only Derby-based supporters that have produced these fanzines, but the Norwegian *NorRam* is still produced and is an excellent quality publication. Other supporters' branches have also produced similar publications, such as the West Country Supporters' Club, the London-based *Capital Ram* and the Australian branch.

The Redoutable Rams – A Pictorial Roll of Honour

Local artist Stuart Avery created an oil painting that currently hangs in a room at Pride Park Stadium, which includes many of the famous players in the history of the club from 1884 through to 1990.

Each player is painted accurately and set against a backdrop of the Baseball Ground, starting with players such as Bloomer and Goodall in the 1890s through to Shilton, Wright and McMinn in the 1990s.

As well as the original, 1,850 limited edition copies were created, which are numbered and signed by the artist and were sold unframed for £30 in 1990.

A separate sheet contained a key to the painting/print showing each player's position and the dates of his playing career at Derby.

Baseball Ground

The 100th anniversary of the first match at the Baseball Ground was commemorated in the match programme dated 21 March 1992 for a Division Two match against Wolverhampton Wanderers. A special supplement was included, covering the statistics, players and cup matches over the 100 years. As part of the celebrations, supporters attending the match could send off for a special 'Attendance Certificate'. There is no information as to how many of these individually-named certificates were produced and one suspects that a large number of them have been lost since then.

A CD-Rom was produced called *Farewell to the Baseball Ground*, which had a digital copy of the book by the same name, the programme from the last match against Arsenal and also various video clips from the original Baseball Ground video.

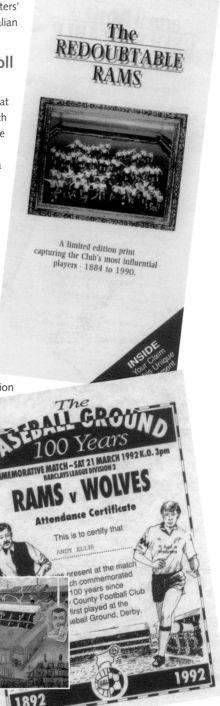

A limited edition print capturing the Club's most influential players · 1884 to 1990.

Plans of the Baseball Ground, showing all the various rooms, have been sold and are quite unique. The drawings open out to form a very large area and show where the police cells were originally located and all the various storerooms and working offices.

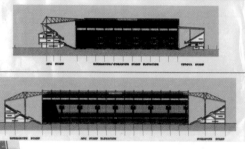

As the stadium was scheduled for redevelopment in 1996, a number of plans of how the stadium was to look are still in existence, and show impressions of the various stands, although the Ley stand was to remain untouched by the developments. A great deal of work went into these plans to build the new stands in a certain order to maximise the attendance and the plans also show what the new stadium would look like as you would approach it from the different side streets.

Other Baseball Ground items produced include badges, both official and unofficial.

The 'End of an Era' badge was unofficial and, to maximise the producer's profit, a number of different combinations of colours were used.

The last official first-team game at the Baseball Ground was against Arsenal on 11 May 1997, and in the previous two home matches (Southampton and Nottingham Forest) leaflets were issued at the turnstiles.

Game 3 – details of Ramtique clearance sale and season ticket information for the new stadium.

A PERSONAL APPEAL FROM DERBY COUNTY'S CHAIRMAN

In the time I've been involved with Derby County Football Club I think I've only made special appeals to you on a handful of occasions.

The plea I am making now though is most important: the world of football will be watching the last ever League game at the Baseball Ground and I want everyone to see the fans of Derby County saying goodbye in the best possible way.

It is important there is no pitch invasion at the end of the Arsenal game — May 11 might be the last League game at the famous ground, but please remember Martin Taylor's Testimonial game will be played at the BBG on May 14 and we have every intention of playing Reserve team games and some Youth team games there next season.

It would be unfortunate and very unfair to Martin — a loyal servant of the club for the past 10 years — if the playing surface was in any way harmed for his game against Everton.

Please remember this is not a situation where the bulldozers are about to move in — the Baseball Ground will continue to play an important part in the life of Derby County.

Also, there is a possibility we will be looking to organise one more big occasion at the old ground before the start of the new season!

If the pitch is clear at the final whistle on May 11, the players will come back for a parade and we have other special features planned.

So please remain in your seats and let's show the watching world of football how Derby County's supporters want to say goodbye to our historic Baseball Ground.

Lionel Pickering

THE LAST LEAGUE GAME AT THE BASEBALL GROUND
Derby County vs Arsenal
11th May 1997

ARSENAL TICKETS
Important Announcement

TICKETS for the last ever League game at Derby County's historic Baseball Ground will now go on sale this Sunday, April 27, and not after tonight's Nottingham Forest game, as originally advertised.

The club has switched the date on security grounds, with the full backing of the police, to prevent queuing problems during and after tonight's game.

Tickets will now go on sale at the Baseball Ground Ticket Office on Sunday from 11.30am — but only to current season ticket holders and fans with a ticket stub from the Forest game. The allocation will be strictly on the basis of one Arsenal ticket per season ticket or Forest ticket stub, and it is not expected that the last game seats will go on general sale.

We apologise to fans for any inconvenience. Please note that due to the anticipated high demand for the Arsenal game, no guarantees can be made that every ticket request will be met.

2 GAMES TO GO AT THE BBG
ROAR 'TIL YOU'RE

JUST 3 MORE,
SO ROAR 'TIL YOU'RE RAW!

DEAR RAMS FAN,

A big thank-you for the fantastic atmosphere you have helped to create at the Baseball Ground — today is the last League Saturday at this famous old ground, so make the most of it.

● Call into the BBG's Sportsman's Lounge from April 18-21 for a 'Farewell To The Baseball Ground' RAMTIQUE CLEARANCE SALE — many great offers including reduced price replica kits. Open Fri 18th & Mon 21st (10am-6pm); Sat 19th & Sun 20th (10am-4pm).

● Season tickets for the New Stadium go on GENERAL SALE on April 21 at the Season Ticket Office at Pride Park, with prices guaranteed at this season's rates until June 1st. Call 01332 672226 for details.

You may have won a full match 'Manchester United vs Rams video with this leaflet: listen out for the half-time announcement

3 GAMES TO GO AT THE BBG
ROAR 'TIL YOU'RE RAW!

DERBY COUNTY FOOTBALL CLUB

Our ref: KAL/MT

7th May 1997

Mr K. Friar,
Managing Director/Secretary,
Arsenal Football Club,
Arsenal Stadium,
Highbury,
London. N5 1BU.

Dear Ken,

re: Derby County v Arsenal
Sunday 11th May 1997

On behalf of my Chairman and Directors, I would like to invite your Chairman, Directors, and wives, to a buffet lunch, at 2 p.m. on Sunday.

Perhaps you would be good enough to confirm who will be attending as soon as possible.

We look forward to seeing you.

Yours sincerely,

Keith

Keith Loring
Chief Executive

DERBY COUNTY FOOTBALL CLUB LIMITED · THE BASEBALL GROUND · DERBY DE23 8NB
TELEPHONE (01332) 340105 · FACSIMILE (01332) 293514

Game 2 – tickets relating to the Arsenal game going on sale on 27 April.

Last game – personal appeal from the chairman not to invade the pitch as still have Martin Taylor testimonial to be played and reserve and youth-team matches in the following years.

There were duplicate tickets produced for the Arsenal game, which are unused and can be purchased. A number of these were sent to Ashley Ward for him to sign, as the last Derby County goalscorer at the Baseball Ground.

Pride Park Stadium

The decision to move to a new stadium was finally taken in February 1996, a matter of days before the proposed redevelopment of the Baseball Ground was to begin. The land available on the City Challenge site had become available following the government's decision to put the Millennium project into London, and Derby moved quickly to secure the land. The opportunity to move to a purpose-built stadium with modern facilities and room to expand was taken.

On 17 November 1996, the foundation stone was laid at the site of the new stadium. Regular leaflets were sent to season-ticket holders as the stadium was built, explaining

the progress and features of the construction.

Supporters were also able to put their 'Name in History' by buying a specially inscribed brick that was to be placed around the outside of the stadium at specially fenced off areas. These cost £35 each and over 3,000 were sold.

The Rams' New Stadium brochure has many details of the stadium inside. The pictures are actually of Middlesbrough's Riverside Stadium, with the seat colours changed from red to black.

The stadium was officially opened by the Queen on 18 July 1997 and a 20-page full-colour brochure was given away on the day

(inside says £2 where sold). These are not difficult to obtain and there were many thousands left over. The first football match was against Italian club Sampdoria on 4 August 1997. As the ticket office was not fully functional at this stage, special tickets were printed and the programme for this first game (32 pages for £1.80) was filled with pictures from the opening. Although these items from the opening match are quite plentiful, they should increase in value over time. The Italian club presented Derby with a 'trophy' of a tower on a marble base.

The first League match was against Wimbledon and had to be abandoned due to a floodlight failure, making the first completed game against Barnsley. Stefano Eranio had the honour of being the first Derby goalscorer at the Rams' new home.

Programmes from the 1990s

There are two versions of the Tottenham Hotspur programme in the 1990–91 season, the ususal matchday edition and an ITV Match edition, printed and distributed throughout the country prior to the game as it was shown live on ITV. This ITV version had an additional outer cover but inside the contents were the same. The price of the programme was £1 for 32 pages.

By 1993–94 the new Bukta kit had introduced a new 'Rams' identification that incorporated the ram's head into the 'R'. This was not only put on the kit, but also on the front cover of the programme, which had undergone a design change to a predominately black cover. The opponents' name was written down the side and the date at the bottom.

A supplement covering the middle

eight pages that gave information about the visitors and also contained the team line-ups was the next major design change to the programme. The cover of the supplement was also reproduced on the front of the main programme. The size had increased to 40 pages and the price increased to £1.40.

Promotion to the Premier League saw an increase in the programme size to 48 pages, but no price increase. Advertising space took up the new pages, as this was easier to sell in the higher Division.

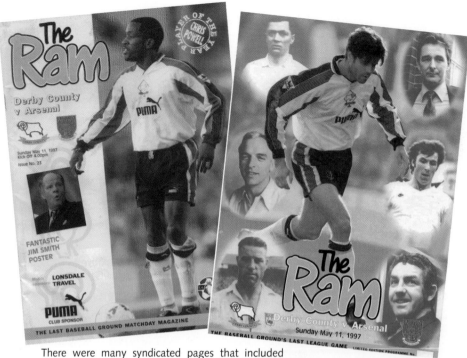

There were many syndicated pages that included statistical graphs and Carling, the League sponsors, took two pages. The teams were no longer numbered 1 to 11 as squad numbering had been introduced, so the line-up page on the back had become a full squad. The value of programmes from this last season at the Baseball Ground has risen, especially for the final game against Arsenal, when there were two editions of the programme, the usual match edition and a limited edition (of 1,000) that was printed on better quality paper and had an additional card cover. The printers' overrun copies, printed to cover losses and damages, were sold at a Programme Fair at Pride Park Stadium later in 1997. These are identifiable as they do not have a number written in the box on the cover.

The programme for the 1999–2000 season won the FPD (Football Programme Directory) Programme of the Year award. While it is always nice to be recognised for winning an award, awards like this and the *Programme Monthly* award are decided by the editor of that publication and come down to personal preferences. Awards presented by institutions such as the CMMA (Commercial and Marketing Managers' Association) carry more prestige.

For the millennium season there were two issues for each programme – the normal match issue and a subscriber-only version. The subscriber version was limited in number to 500 and, although the programme content was identical, the paper quality was much higher and there was a gold stamp on the cover reading 'Millennium Gold Collection', and other areas were printed in gold. These sets were also distributed with a team sheet for each game and the result sheet showing the results and current League table after the game. Although there was a maximum of 500 sets, far fewer than this were actually ordered and the others have been sold to various dealers. The first match of the new millennium, against Watford on 3 January 2000, saw a special edition of the programme called the Platinum Limited Edtion . This was a Millennium Gold edition with an additional platinum cover that was blank on the inside. On the back of the cover, an individual number was printed. These issues were originally made available to season-ticket holders only.

Season tickets

The large, square-shape book was eventually replaced by a shorter and wider version. The one shown is from the last season at the Baseball Ground in 1996–97.

SEASON TICKET 1995-96

The move to Pride Park Stadium introduced further new technology into the club and the tickets, in the form of special ram logo holograms printed onto them.

With the club in the Premier League and many matches, at home and away, being made all-ticket, the demand for away match tickets was such that away season tickets were available for those that wished to guarantee their ticket to the away fixtures.

Subbuteo kits

In 1991 Derby were given their own kit again, this time reference 722, which came in different formats, one for 1991 and an updated one in 1992–93. Being in the Second Division meant that by 1994 the unique identity was lost and the Derby playing kit was switched to number 156, along with any team playing in white shirts and black shorts. They remained on this number through to the end of the official Subbuteo range in 1996.

Hasbro then bought out the original Subbuteo

SEASON TICKET 1996-97

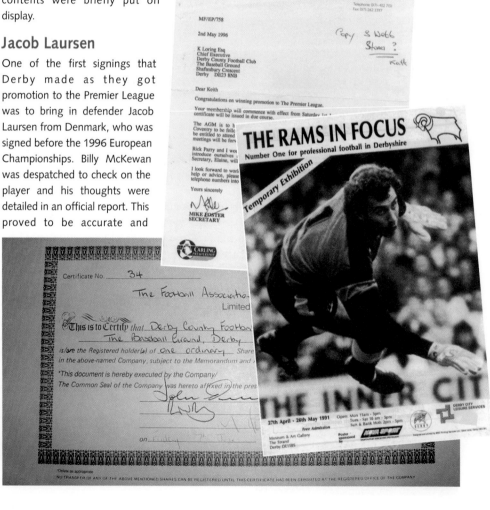

and cut back on the range and variants of club colours available, although getting promotion to the Premier League meant that exclusive kits were again manufactured. The first of these, number 63027, was the kit that was used in the promotion season in 1995–96 and also the first year in the Premier League. The second of these was 63336, also with the Puma logo on the front.

Rams in Focus

The 'Rams in Focus' exhibition in April and May 1991 was held at the City Museum and was the first time many of the club's artefacts had been brought together. The time capsule that was buried at the Osmaston End of the Baseball Ground was put together containing such items as playing kits, books, Subbuteo teams, scarves, programmes and newspapers. This was dug up in 2003 as the old stadium was demolished and the contents were briefly put on display.

Jacob Laursen

One of the first signings that Derby made as they got promotion to the Premier League was to bring in defender Jacob Laursen from Denmark, who was signed before the 1996 European Championships. Billy McKewan was despatched to check on the player and his thoughts were detailed in an official report. This proved to be accurate and detailed enough to make Jim Smith buy the player.

Stadium models

In 1993 the first model of the Baseball Ground was produced by JPH Design. This was a cardboard box that contained cut out and stick models of the stands, floodlights and executive box complex. When the box is upturned, each stand can be placed in its correct position to form the stadium. Once built, there is not a great deal one can do with it and being made of card it is unlikely that many survive today.

Premier Collectables produced a model of Pride Park Stadium in two versions, one that was completed and one as a kit that you were able to paint yourself.

There are large-scale models of the Baseball Ground and Pride Park that are regularly seen, and these were built by father-and-son team Steve and Christopher Hudson. The scale used is 2mm:1ft, which is the 'N' gauge used in model railways. Both models are made of balsa wood, tick card and wooden dowel for the stadium structure and model railway grass material for the pitches. The models were built on and off during evenings, and the Baseball Ground took 14 months to put together and Pride Park 34 months between December 1993 and August 2001.

DERBY COUNTY FOOTBALL CLUB
BASEBALL GROUND DERBY DE3 8NB   0821

From: BILLY McEWAN

Date 8TH AUG 1995
Player JACOB LAURSEN
Position CENTRAL DEFENDER
Club SILKEBORG.
Match v. CRUSADERS
Age
Height 5'9 - 5'10
Weight LOOKS AROUND 12ST.
General Build GOOD STRONG SHAPE.
Any Special Remarks

REPORT

PACE — AVERAGE. (BUT WAS NEVER CAUGHT OUT AT BACK)

COURAGE. — NOT AFRAID TO PUT A FOOT IN, OR DIDN'T DUCK OUT OF MUCH IN AIR.

PASSING — GOOD 1ST TOUCH AND VERY COMFORTABLE ON BALL. LONG PASSING VERY GOOD.

VISION & AWARENESS VERY GOOD AND READS GAME WELL.

TEMPERANT. APPARENTLY WHEN HE WAS YOUNGER WAS A BIT OF A FIERY LAD (ERIC THE AGENT TELLS ME) BUT HAS SETTLED DOWN AND TONIGHT SHOWED GOOD COMPOSURE IN A HOSTILE ATMOSPHERE ACCEPTS RESPONSIBILITY

THE LAD PLAYED WELL TONIGHT (BEARING IN MIND THE OPPOSITION) (COMFORTABLE ON BALL AND NOT AFRAID TO GO AND JOIN IN ATTACKS IF HE FEELS IT'S ON TO DO SO. R/FOOTED (VERY GOOD). BUT CAN USE 2/FOOT AS WELL. HE'S ON BALL AT ALL 7/KICKS AND PLACES A GOOD SHOT AS HE DEMONSTRATED TONIGHT BY HITTING THE POST TONIGHT. NOT THE BIGGEST FOR A CRACK BUT WILL COMPETE FOR BALL IN AIR. AND RECOVERY RUNS COULD BE QUICKER BUT FAIRLY MOBILE. AND MORE MATCHES COULD GET THIS. ON THIS ONE MATCH TONIGHT. I LIKE WHAT I SAW

Ground Conditions DRY & BIT BUMPY.

FOR CLUB USE ONLY

IN POSSESSION OF BALL
27 TIMES
(GOOD PASSES 18
BAD " 9)

HEADERS
13   4 BAD
          9 GOOD

Signed BM Ewan

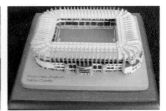

Royal Crown Derby

Royal Crown Derby produced a ram in a special colourway commissioned by the club that was the same as the usual ram marketed except that the blue colour in the coat became black and the leaves around the base were a different colour. Standing 8cm high, it also had the Derby County logo on the backstamp, the familiar gold stopper and a certificate containing the signatures of Hugh Gibson (Royal Crown Derby) and Lionel Pickering. It was introduced in 1998 and has not been made since 1999. These are highly collectable by Royal Crown Derby enthusiasts.

Mercury phone cards

1990–91 saw the release of Mercurycards, which were actually telephone cards that could be used on the Mercury network. There are many collectors of such cards, but these never really caught on. They were available to purchase individually at

£2 (team picture on the front) and £5 (team badge on the front). A limited edition set of 4,000 had both cards in a presentation folder. Very few of these numbered packs were sold and the majority were destroyed, making those that survive now very collectable.

Autographed items

The trend for autographed items really began in the late 1990s when players would sign photographs in the Ramtique in the days before Christmas, and you could often find signed magazine pictures and programmes signed by the players and squad.

The demands placed on football clubs to produce a seemingly never-ending supply of goods for raffles and charitable auctions led to an autographed football being sent to these events. From being quite rare and sought after, there is now a constant supply on the internet and they can be purchased quite cheaply.

Initially, proper match balls were used and the example shows the signatures of Arthur Cox, Trevor Hebberd, Craig Ramage and Peter Shilton, who was not reknowned for signing items during his playing career. These early balls are only signed using a ball-point pen, so over time these will fade or rub off, whereas the modern ones use a permanent marker pen.

By the end of the decade, special balls had been produced for this purpose, some carrying the Pride Park or Rammie logos. The example dates from the 1997–98 season, the first at Pride Park. Although the date is not on the ball at all, some detective work on the signatures shows it was signed by Chris Powell, who left Derby at the end of that season.

One of the main issues with the footballs is that they need a large amount of room to be displayed and one can only see a small proportion of the signatures at any one time.

Club kit

The partnership with Umbro continued into the 1990s with the sponsor changing to Auto Windscreens.

Bukta were the next supplier and their radical design made the shirt into a baseball-style with pin-stripe lines and black sleeves, and also changed the direction the ram was facing. The away kit was an horrendous combination of black, blue and white stripes that varied in width. Bukta ceased trading after the first year of the contract and a 'Rams Pro Wear' patch was put over the Bukta label.

The cover of the 1995–96 merchandising catalogue carried a picture of the kit for the coming two

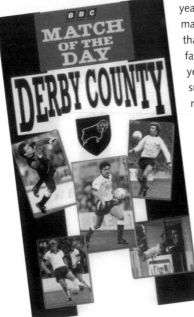

years, which was produced by Puma, who were also the club's main sponsor. The quality of the Puma shirts was much better than shirts from previous years and they were the firm favourite of the fans. The away kit was changed after the first year to become a Heart of Midlothian purple, liked by many supporters. Puma continued as the main kit supplier for the remainder of the decade.

Media

Many videos were released during the 1990s that consisted of compilations, full matches or season highlights. The BBC, with its vast archives of *Match of the Day* footage, released a compilation of the highlights in 1992 and covered many of the famous televised matches since 1964.

Following on from the success of various historical Derby County books, Anton Rippon produced a video called *The Derby County Story* in 1993. It was an

expensive video, originally costing £14.99 for the 60-minute film.

A further compilation, *Match of the '70s*, put together the goals and highlights from many of the famous matches during that time, including the Benfica and Real Madrid matches and the 12–0 record score against Finn Harps. This has been remastered and reissued in DVD format.

With the success of the book *Farewell to the Baseball Ground*, a company called CD-Archives digitally photographed it and created a CD called *The Last Goodbye*. The CD also included the programme from the last Baseball Ground match against Arsenal and various video clips taken from a Baseball Ground video produced in 1997.

Chapter Ten
2000-2005

A victory against Champions Manchester United in the last away game of the 2000–01 season secured another year in the Premier League. This came after a disastrous start that didn't see a League win until mid-November. Taribo West was recruited on a short-term loan and immediately results started to improve.

A string of poor signings by Jim Smith and a constant changing of formation, new players and different coaches led to a season-long struggle.

The close-season months of 2002 were dominated by the attempts to sign Fabrizio Ravanelli and, despite scoring on his debut, he was unable to stop another poor start to the season. This eventually forced the resignation of Jim Smith, allowing his assistant and former Derby player Colin Todd to take full-time charge. His stay was brief as results continued to be poor, the team being permanently in the bottom three for nearly all of the season. John Gregory left Aston Villa and was almost immediately appointed as Todd's successor. Despite bringing in some experienced players (Rob Lee and Warren Barton), he was unable to fight off the inevitable relegation that had been likely for a couple of seasons. Sections of the supporters blamed the chairman for not allowing further signings, but the one signing of Ravanelli at the expense of two or three other players rests with the manager.

With the club now in the First Division and weighed down with Premiership wages and falling attendances, there were inevitable financial problems. The club was in need of a financial injection, which caused a split in the board room. Despite stories of various consortia being interested, nothing formal was put forward to rescue the club. Money-spinning cup runs were unheard of and injuries forced Derby to field 15-year old Lee Holmes in the FA Cup tie at Brentford. He became the youngest player ever to play in the competition. Gregory was then suspended by the club for unspecified irregularities and George Burley was appointed as a temporary replacement. A late run of good results and new confidence pulled the club to a respectable position, but with finances getting worse the star players (Poom, Riggott, Carbonari, Christie, Higginbotham, Burley and Ravanelli) were gradually sold or had their contracts paid-up to help reduce running costs.

Burley was officially appointed as full-time manager by the start of the 2003–04 season but had few players to choose from and brought in loan players to make up a team. Many of these players were untried reserve players from Premiership clubs who came in for spells of between one and three months. It also gave a chance for home-grown Academy players to break into the team and one of them, Tom Huddlestone, played for most of the season despite having played only a few reserve-team matches. Eventually, with the club facing bankruptcy, a new three-man board of directors, none of whom were recognised Derby supporters, or even known in the city, took control from Lionel Pickering and got a grip on the finances and organisation of the club. New experienced players started to arrive in the New Year and home form became the club's saviour as they won eight out of the last 11 matches. Having survived relegation by one point and one place the club was hoping for better fortunes.

Backed by season ticket sales of 17,700, the stated aim was to finish in the top half of the table and early season results certainly pointed to that. Close-season signings of Konjic, Bisgaard, Smith and Idiakez boosted the squad. An early-season injury to Konjic forced Huddlestone into the back four, and while he was adapting to the role many goals were conceded and points thrown away, particularly at home. The arrival of Polish striker Rasiak saw the Rams climb the table dramatically and equal a club record of six successive away League wins and 12 overall. The home form gradually improved and the play-offs were reached by finishing in fourth place, the highest finish for nine years. With top scorer Rasiak and playmaker Idiakez missing through an injury from the first leg Derby were eliminated at the semi-final stages of the play-offs by Preston North End.

Soon afterwards, manager George Burley resigned and left for Hearts, being replaced by Phil Brown, the Bolton Wanderers assistant manager. With Burley taking many of the backroom staff with him and a number of players leaving at the end of their contracts, Brown was faced with a difficult first few months in management.

Books

Ian Hall's *Voices of the Rams* was published in 2000, and in this book he interviews a number of past and present players, managers, directors, media, supporters and club staff on various footballing subjects. *The Legends of Derby County* lists the author's top 100 players and managers during the club's history. There are two pages per person, one a full-page photograph and the other a narrative on his contribution. While not everyone will agree with his choices, it does make interesting reading and is an ageless discussion topic.

Michael Cockayne's first book, *The Clough Years* (2003), looks at key matches of each season, which are examined in detail, while the appendix contains the team line-ups for every Clough-managed game.

Champions 1974–75 (2004) takes us through the 1974–75 season on a match-by-match basis from the pre-season matches through UEFA Cup games to the last match against Carlisle United, with details compiled from contemporary newspaper reports, programmes and personal recollections. It was published in time to mark the 30th anniversary of the Rams last League Championship win. His latest work, *Derby County: A Season by Season History* (2005) recounts the history of the club, highlighting the highs and lows, transfers, politics and personalities, and is lavishly illustrated.

The Official Diary of the Season 2003–04, is jointly published by the *Derby Evening Telegraph* and First Edition (who have also produced similar books with other newspapers) and uses the match reports of its chief sports writer Steve Nicholson along with statistics to provide a different view of each match played during a difficult season for the club. There are two pages for every game played, with a match report, full statistics for both teams and the other results that day.

Another recent Derby manager to have gone into print is Jim Smith in *It's Only a Game*, which updates a previous autobiography and was completed while he was still manager at Pride Park. Over one third of the book relates to his time at Derby, which by any standards was eventful, with a large turnover of players, promotion in his first season, an influx of foreign players and the move from the Baseball Ground to Pride Park. It gives an interesting view from inside the dressing room.

This book, *Relics of the Rams: The Hidden Treasures of Derby County*, has been compiled with the help of many collectors from around the globe and features many of the trophies and items within the club as well as the many collectable objects accumulated by the Derby fans. Some of these have either not been seen for many years, or have never been seen publicly before, having been stored in a collection and viewed by only a few people.

More recently, Dave Mackay has written his second autobiography, the first having been printed way back in the early 1960s soon after Tottenham Hotspur won the double. This new book includes his time at Derby, firstly arriving as a player and then returning as manager, amid calls for players' strikes and the return of Clough and Taylor.

Other former players to go into print in the last few years are Peter Shilton, Charlie George and

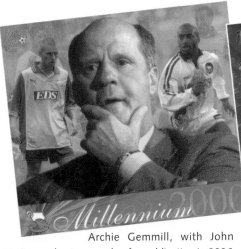

Archie Gemmill, with John McGovern having one due for publication in 2006.

Since the 2003–04 season the club has issued a season-ticket holders' handbook that combines ticket holder information with features usually found in a typical yearbook, such as club directory, fixture lists, player profiles and commercial information.

Cards and stickers

A new name in card production, Futera, marked the millennium with a special 18-card set that was available with Chupa Chups sweets. These cards were also available in a special leather binder (limited to 450 only, and known as the Platinum set), with each card occupying a separate page, gilded in 22 carat gold. A numbered, larger centrepiece card was issued. The 8x7in centrepiece cards were also available separately in a limited edition of 900 cards.

Topps (the trade card division of Merlin) continued their association with the Premier League and introduced various 'chase' cards. These are very limited in number and, in some way, unique. Mart Poom, the Estonian goalkeeper, seemed to get most attention, having a special match-worn shirt card and also an autographed card that were part of these chase cards.

Merlin also produced the usual

stickers, venturing into autographed editions where all the stickers had printed autographs of the players on them

Wizard of the Coast produced a card game for the 2001–02 season, similar to the Top Trumps and Subbuteo games from the 1970s and 1990s, featuring 17 Derby players, with an additional 'Title Race' top-up set produced later in the season. Special foil-finish cards featuring Powell, Christie and

Burton were also part of the set, these being more valuable than the standard cards.

An anonymous cigarette card-style print has been produced called 'Derby County Unforgettables' and features 16 players from Steve Bloomer through to Kinkladze.

Programmes

One of the biggest complaints among collectors about modern programmes became more obvious during the first few years of the new millennium. Some clubs decided to try different sizes and formats and West Bromwich Albion, in particular, decided that quantity was better than quality and produced 100-page editions for each game. On closer inspection, there is lots of white space on each page and many pages containing single pictures, while of course there is more space for advertising content.

For general issues, programmes were of such a size and quality that normal programme binders were no longer big enough for the storage of the programmes. This is becoming an increasing issue with

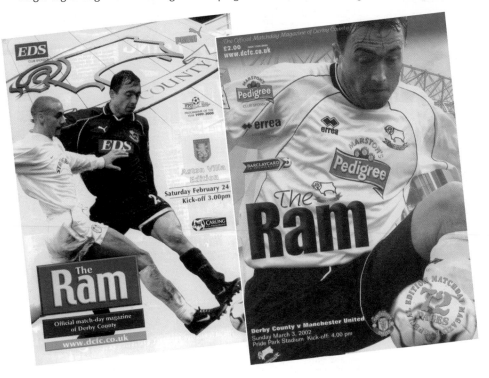

dealers and many are no longer willing to supply current season programmes due to the storage space required and the postage costs involved. The old-fashioned idea of a match programme has now been replaced by what has become a fortnightly club magazine. The cost of these productions is also an issue for younger supporters and a probable reason why youngsters are not collecting programmes in the numbers that they used to.

The programme cover for the 2000–01 season became cluttered with various logos for match sponsor, kit sponsor, League sponsor, the opposing team badge and the Programme of the Year 1999–2000 logo from the Football Programme Directory organisation (FPD). The background remained the same for each issue, a large ram logo, but the action picture changed. The programme had increased to a point where a separate page just for the programme contents was required, and there was also one for a directory of relevant staff and phone numbers. The price was £2 for 64 pages.

The last match of the 2002–03 season saw a special Brian Clough edition to mark him receiving the freedom of the City on 4 May 2003 against Ipswich Town. There was also a limited edition of 1,000 numbered copies that were printed on superior quality paper and had a number printed on the front cover.

Although the pre-season friendly programme of 2004–05 (v Aston Villa) was produced by the previous contractors, a deal was struck with Dunwoody Sports Marketing that meant that the production costs were taken over by them, with the result that any unsold copies were taken back after each game. There were some issues that were in short supply and also some that sold out on the day of the game. No dealers, unless they were pre-ordered, have any spare copies of Derby programmes, and this may push prices higher for some issues. Each programme had a standard banner and close-up picture of a player, with the usual logos in one place. An additional logo for this season is that to mark the 30th anniversary of the last Championship win in 1974–75.

As well as the match programme, there are hundreds of teamsheets produced for each game. These were originally produced for the VIPs and press, showing the actual teams playing, but are now produced for all of the restaurant and executive areas and have become an advertising medium as well as listing the teams and officials. Because of their limited availability to the general public, there are not many collectors of these pieces of paper, but they are something different.

With the size of the playing squads and the number of teams that have to be prepared for the start of a new season, the club is often inundated with requests for pre-season friendly matches and it is not unknown for the club to field teams for matches played on the same day. An example is from 3 August 2000, where the first team played KSTVV and at the same time played at Hayes. Interestingly, Richard Jackson, Paul Boertien and Adam Murray are listed as substitutes for the game in Belgium and in the starting line-up against Hayes. Some of these pre-season friendly matches are not as well publicised as they might be and this can lead to a shortage of programmes among collectors.

Lee Holmes became the youngest-ever player to appear in an FA Cup match (and also Derby's youngest player, beating Steve Powell) when he made an appearance as the third substitute in the Derby team that lost at Brentford in January 2003. The programme does not even list him in the squad, which goes up to 41. He actually wore the number 44 for the remainder of the season. making a further two substitute appearances. Fifty copies of the match programme were signed by the player and put on sale on a first-come, first-served basis and they will increase in value over time.

Rampage magazine

The club, like many others, began production of its own magazine, which was available through the newsagent network as well as being given to season-ticket holders. First produced in the autumn of 1997, it continued for 21 issues until the summer of 2002 when relegation and mounting costs saw its end. Throughout its time, it provided more in-depth player interviews than the usual match programme allowed and could also carry articles, competitions and pictures that would not suit the matchday programme. It varied in size, starting at a normal magazine size and ending up a large 13x9½in (the idea behind the large size was to make it stand out on the newsagents' shelves), making it too large to handle on matchdays and too big to store alongside other magazines and programmes.

Club kit

The shirts used at the start of the decade were manufactured by Puma, the renowned sportswear supplier from Germany who had been the supplier since 1995. The quality of their replica shirts and other sportswear was excellent. The home kit had a V-neck with multiple black stripes around the collar and was predominately white, with a big EDS logo of the main sponsor.

The scheduled change of kit in 2001 saw the supplier switched to the Italian company Errea, and the kit went back to a round neck with single black trim, similar to the late 1960s, although there was extra piping on the shirt.

The away kit was a combination of light and dark blue shirts and light blue shorts and was not one of the fans' favourites.

The 2003 version of the shirt was slightly changed around the collar and the black piping was different and less obtrusive on the white shirt.

The Errea deal having finished, the new kit manufacturers were the Spanish company Joma and a new club sponsor, the Derbyshire Building Society, was announced at the same time. The main difference in the home kit was the prominent black stripe down the front of the shirt.

Last matches

The last away matches of the 2003–04 (v Wimbledon) and 2004–05 (v Coventry City) seasons were unique special occasions for the home teams. It was to be the last game that Wimbledon would play with that name, changing to the Milton Keynes Dons during the summer. The programme for this game was a sell-out on the day and the all-ticket, travelling support outnumbered the home

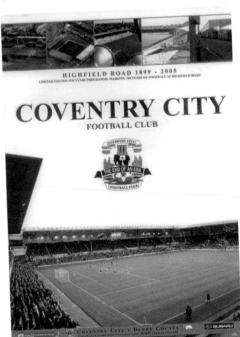

supporters. The Coventry City game was an emotional event as this was the last League match to be played at the Highfield Road stadium, and as well as a capacity crowd there are many items to commemorate the match. The normal matchday programme was expanded to a 132-page publication costing £6, and there was also a limited edition, numbered version of 2,500 that were personally signed by the Coventry chairman and cost £10. Four different types of badge were produced with an 'I was There!' logo and details of the match, with one of them being an unusual ticket shape. The quality of these badges, however, is not high.

To complete the Derby connection, a special first-day cover was printed for the day, and all of these are sure to be highly collectable, certainly by Coventry fans, in the future. All of these items could be pre-ordered from Coventry so Derby fans could have obtained them without too much difficulty.

Media

Modern video technology now allows the production of match-by-match DVDs, with all the sophisticated editing and slow motion techniques. The club now has its own tv/video editing suite and production for matches, season reviews and compilations on DVD has increased.

A video about the Baseball Ground was first produced when the club moved to Pride Park in 1997, and as the final closure date approached, it was re-released with the addition of a number of interviews with former players. An updated version called *The Final Chapter* was produced in 2005 and included the final demolition of the stadium.

With the power and affordability of modern computers there is now a market for specific computer games and products. *Club Manager 2005* is a computer game where you become the manager of the team, starting with the current playing squad. Filled with player profiles, pictures and downloadable updates from the internet, the game can be kept up-to-date with player transfers during the season. However, it does not rank highly among football manager simulation games, which are dominated by *Football Manager*, *Championship Manager* and *FIFA* football games.

Last days of the Baseball Ground

Reserve and youth-team matches continued to be played at the Baseball Ground until the end of the 2002–03 season, when the stadium was sold to the Walbrook Group.

The last reserve-team game played was against Watford on 20 August 2002, and the last official Derby County game played at the stadium was an Under-19 match against Newcastle United on 19 April 2003, both of which had the usual photocopied teamsheet. The team for the Under-19 game included Lee Holmes and Tom Huddlestone, who have gone on to play for the first team. Huddlestone has won England Under-21 caps and made a lucrative transfer to Tottenham Hotspur at the end of the 2004–05 season.

The very last game was a supporters' match in May where individuals bid for a place in the team. This game was preceeded by an ex-Rams match that saw Kevin Hector, Roger Davies and David Nish making their last appearances.

In the months leading up to the handing over of the

Farewell Tours
2003

stadium, various items were sold off by public auction to supporters. These included turnstiles, various advertising signs, individual plastic seats, football books and documents.

Naturally, the club retained the more important parts of the stadium, including the last set of wooden seats from the back row of the Osmaston Lower tier (see 1930s), the clock (see 1960s), the physiotherapists' bench and some of the internal doors from the changing rooms and the padded boardroom door.

Other unique items are a sign from the 'B' Stand indicating seat numbers, a ticket board that used to hang above the turnstile entrances showing the season ticket number for the current match and the sign at the end of the player's tunnel showing the direction of the various dressing rooms. One item that has added significance since the death of Brian Clough in 2004 is the 'Manager' door sign from the Manager's Office. During his last tour of the Baseball Ground on his Freedom of the City day in 2003, he stopped and autographed this sign, which is on display at Pride Park.

Behind the scenes tours also took place on Sundays, for which a four-page tour guide was given away to those attending the pre-booked event.

Trophies

Some of the other items that can regularly be seen on display at Pride Park include the Derbyshire Football Association Centenary Cup, which has mainly been contested between Derby County and Chesterfield since 1983.

The home match during the 2003–04 season against local rivals Nottingham Forest will be remembered not only for the 4–2 scoreline, but also for Derby's second goal, scored by Paul Peschisolido when the Nottingham Forest goalkeeper allowed a back pass to hit a plastic coffee cup and his subsequent miskick gave him a tap-in for a goal. The cup was rescued by the stewards and was signed by the player and appeared on various T-shirts and mugs.

The Jack Stamps Memorial Trophy, more commonly known as the Player of the Year trophy, is housed in the boardroom trophy cabinets.

Signed items

The demand for signed footballs has been replaced by autographed replica shirts, which are easier to look after and can be mounted and framed in such a way as to show off all the signatures.

With many foreign players coming into the game, there are different ways of signing autographs and after a period of time it is not possible to work out which signature belongs to which player. Where possible, you should try and identify the signatures as they are collected. The squad system has meant that a player is assigned a squad number at the start of the season and in many cases a signature is accompanied by this number for identification purposes.

With many of the players having personal sponsorships for parts of the kit, such as boots or gloves for the goalkeepers, they are more willing to sign these and let them go. Stefano Eranio signed a number of his football boots when he left Derby to return to Italy, and Mart Poom has also signed pairs of his match-worn gloves.

Internationals

Although the Baseball Ground staged a full England international match against Ireland on 11 February 1911 as well as the occasional schoolboy international, Derby was largely overlooked as an international venue, despite its central location. Derby's rise to the top of the English game, coupled with having a number of Under-23 players, meant Derby was able to stage its first Under-23 international match in February 1972 against Scotland.

The move to Pride Park, with modern facilities, encouraged the Football Association to give Derby an Under-21 International against France on 9 February 1999. A record-breaking crowd for an Under-21 match saw Derby produce two versions of the programme, the match edition and also a Silver Issue Limited Edition that was numbered on the cover and was sold with a laminated teamsheet from the game.

The England bandwagon returned on 6 October 2000 for a European Championship Qualifier against Germany, and the 36-page programme cost £2. Programme production had been taken over by the Football Association and this is one of the rarest modern Under-21 programmes. Sales were underestimated and the programme was a sell-out, with no spare copies going to the dealers.

While Wembley Stadium was being rebuilt, the England team had a policy of playing around the country at as many different suitable stadia as possible. Pride Park was the best and biggest in the East Midlands, and the big night came in May 2001 when the full England team played Mexico in a friendly international. The whole of the stadium and football club was taken over by the Football Association and advertising boards, programmes, various tradesmen and fans from around the country came to town. The influx of people from outside the city meant that many special signs were put up around the city directing traffic to specific parking areas and afterwards many people removed these and kept them.

The usual A4-size brochure/programme cost a massive £4 and there is also a press and VIP teamsheet available.

Two further Under-21 matches were played at Pride Park, both against Holland. One came in November 2001 as the European Championship play-off and the second was in February 2005 in a friendly.

The quality of the programmes produced by the Football Association is not very good and they are expensive, costing £2 for 28 pages, of which nine are adverts.

Match tickets from any England game are keenly sought after and worth hanging on to, particularly the Mexico one.

Useful contacts

Derby County Football Club
Pride Park Stadium
Pride Park
Derby
DE248XL
Tel: 0870 444 1884
www.dcfc.co.uk

The National Football Museum
Sir Tom Finney Way,
Deepdale,
Preston,
PR1 6RU.
www.nationalfootballmuseum.com

Paul Booth Sporting Memorabilia
10 Gayton Avenue
Littleover
Derby
DE23 1GA
Email:paulbooth_bruce@hotmail.com
Tel: 01332 770034

Graham Budd Auctions Ltd.
In association with Sotheby's
Po Box47519
London
N14 6XD
E-Mail: gb@grahambuddauctions.co.uk
Tel/fax: 020 8366 2525
www.grahambuddauctions.co.uk

Christies
85 Old Brompton Road
London
SW7 3LD
Tel: +44 (0)20 7930 6074

Mike Heard Cigarette Card Specialist
2 Ferrers Way
Darley Abbey
Derby
DE22 2AA
Email : sportingutopia@aol.com
Tel: 01332 558037

Barry Heather/Derby Trading Cards
Indoor Market, Eagle Centre or
16 Rosedale Avenue
Allenton
Derby
DE24 0FJ
Email: Barry.heather@ntlworld.com
Tel: 01332 733859

Brian Johnson/Almondvale Programmes
5 Albion Road
Edinburgh
EH7 5QJ
Tel:0131 652 1444
www.almondvaleprogrammes.com

Programme Monthly
46 Milton Road
Kirkcaldy
Fife
KY11TL
Email:progm@hotmail.com
www.pmfc.co.uk

Royal Crown Derby Visitor Centre
194 Osmaston Road
Derby
DE23 8JZ
Tel:01332 712800
www.royalcrownderby.co.uk

TOFFS
PO Box 71
Gateshead
Tyne and Wear
NE11 0UZ
Email:enquiries@toffs.com
Tel: 08450 6 1966 6

Chris Williams/Sporting Memorabilia
2 Red Lion Drive
Stokenchurch
Buckinghamshire
HP14 3SR
Email: cjw@sportingmem.co.uk
Tel: 01494 485209
www.sportingmem.co.uk